THE EDGE OF THE WORLD

Next Stop Cape Horn

CORAL WAIGHT

Copyright © 2018 Coral Waight

Coral Waight has asserted her right under the Copyright, Designs and Patents Act 1988 to be identified as the author of this work. The information in this book is based on the author's experiences and opinions. The publisher specifically disclaims responsibility for any adverse consequences, which may result from use of the information contained herein. Permission to use information has been sought by the author. Any breaches will be rectified in further editions of the book.

All rights are reserved. No part of this publication may be reproduced, stored in or introduced into a retrieval system, or transmitted in any form, or by any means (electronic, mechanical, photocopying, recording or otherwise) without the prior written permission of the author.

ISBN: 978-0-6483364-0-2 (paperback)
Prepublication Data available from The National Library of Australia.

Cover image by Coral Waight
Cover design by Busybird Publishing

Other books in the *Planning to the Nth* series
Hangi, Haka and Hobbits: Notes from New Zealand
Is This the Road to Stratford?

The Edge of the World (poem) published with kind permission of Brian Inder

Contents

July 2006	i
July 2009	58
October 2009	120
March 2012	167
About the Author	241

The Edge of the World – Next Stop Cape Horn

July 2006

Prologue

It's four o'clock and I'm thinking I should ring the tourist park at Strahan to say I'm running late. There's no mobile coverage but it's been allowed for. A public phone stands at the side of the road just outside the town of Tullah.

'Be here by six,' the woman answers, 'we leave then.'

I've looked at the map and there's not too far to go.

'No worries. I'll make it easily.'

I drive another hour and it's nearly dark. People, on the whole, are not practical when giving advice on travelling. No-one told me Tasmania was dark at five o'clock in winter. I needed to know that. I'm not sure how much longer my concentration will hold out. It's been a huge day. I left the *Spirit of Tasmania*, the ferry that brought me and my little hatch-back across Bass Strait from Melbourne to Devonport, around 7 am. Everyone else on the ship disappeared within minutes, while I drove in circles looking for somewhere for breakfast. I know it's Sunday and I know it was early but surely some enterprising soul with a cafe this close to the ferry terminal could open for people like me on their first jaunt to 'Tassie'.

Just before giving up I saw a cafe that had been there all along and I realised how tired I was. I'd had a cabin to myself but kept waking up, not wanting to miss anything of my first trip, on a ship, into an ocean. Eggs and bacon in front of an open fire energised me and I set out on my adventure. My travel-agent daughter suggested I pass through Sheffield, a country town with the history of the area painted in murals on the walls of the buildings. She also strongly recommended a walk around Dove Lake, which lies at the feet of the great dolomite crags of Cradle Mountain. I don't think she meant me to do it all on the first day.

I've done road trips before so I'm not a complete novice when it comes to distances but I don't seem to be getting anywhere. I left Cradle hours ago. Maybe I took a wrong turn. There's nothing here but mountains and forests; mile after mile of corners to navigate in the dark. Now and then an SUV roars past and I watch its tail-lights disappear into the gloom. They obviously know where they're going; *I* haven't got a clue. I could be here forever, alone, driving into a black eternity. Enough of the melodrama; must pull myself together; must concentrate. What if I don't make it in time? What if they close up and leave me stranded?

It's twenty to six and I see a couple of lights off in the distance. Civilization, maybe. A house; a sign; more signs. I've reached the outskirts of Strahan. I drive around a corner past a cabin park, not mine, and up the dimly lit main street. In fact, it's so dim I can't make out anything clearly. Peering through the windscreen, I reach the top of the hill, realise I've gone too far and turn back. I drive from one end of town to the other – twice. My tourist park does not exist. The pub – they'll know.

'Nope,' says the barman, 'never heard of it.' Mustn't cry; I have to find a bed for the night before I cry.

'That's it,' says the girl at the general store, pointing to the park opposite, the one I've driven past three times.

'But the sign says a different name.'

'I know,' she says, 'but that's it.'

I drive down the side street, turn right into a lane and right again, looking for 'Reception'. The park is in darkness, there seem to be no occupants and there is no 'Reception'. Something happens to my brain when I'm stressed, it switches and everything becomes muddled, just for the moment. Maybe that's what's happened. Maybe I'm looking straight at 'Reception' and can't see it.

'You want something?' says a man, striding past the front of my stationary car. I sag with relief.

'I'm looking for "Reception".'

'Over there!'

'Where?' He throws his arm up.

'Near the light pole,' he barks and marches away. I head back to the lane. There is no 'Reception' at the light pole but a dim light issues from the porch of a white house further along. 'Office' says the small sign over the door.

'Oh, my God, I couldn't find you!' The woman behind the counter stares at me. 'I've been driving for hours. I thought you might have left.'

'Where have you come from?'

'Dove Lake. I thought I'd never get here. It took over three hours.'

'It takes one and a half. I've just come from there.' Mustn't cry; not yet.

'You've got a different name on your sign. I drove past thinking it was the wrong place.' I could have been talking to the wall.

'You're in 9,' she says, slapping the keys on the counter. 'It's the next drive on the right. There's a heater going so it should be warm.' Well, that's something. I'm squinting through the windscreen at the darkened cabins, searching for Number 9 when my mobile rings.

'How'd you go?' It's my travel agent daughter.

'I couldn't find the town and I couldn't find the park and I can't find my cabin and they're so rude and it's all mountains and it's *so* dark. There's something wrong with the lighting.'

'Mum,' she says, 'you *are* in the wild west, you know.'

'Right, yes, right. Here I am! Number 9! I've found it! I'll ring you back when I get in.'

I *am* in the wild west. Some mental adjustment is needed. I now understand the worried look on her face when I announced I was doing the west coast first.

'Rubbish,' say the locals in the general store when I question the timing of the trip from Dove Lake. 'It's a good two and a quarter, *if* you know your way.' Relieved I'm not totally mad, I grab my chips and some milk and cereal for the morning and wander back across the road, down the side street and along the lane.

The Edge of the World – Next Stop Cape Horn

Chapter 1

I've always wanted to explore Tasmania. I wanted to learn more about the place where many of the convicts transported here by the British Government, worked out their sentences. I also wanted to see the forests that were considered so precious they were on the *World Heritage List*. I'm not a good travelling companion. I'm bored by shopping, restaurants, wineries and art galleries but I can sit in a town square for two hours watching the locals going about their business. I can spend the same amount of time in a forest gazing at a stream making its way down a hill or straining my neck to see the top of a 600-year-old tree. I like travelling alone because it gives me full say in where I go, how long I spend in each place and what I do when I'm there.

Tassie is easy to get to from where I live in Melbourne, and easy to drive around, and yet, other than a drive from Hobart to Burnie with someone who considered stopping to look at anything an unnecessary irritation, I'd never made the trip. My family must have been sick of hearing about it because, on my 60th birthday, they presented me with a ticket for the crossing and five nights' accommodation. I added a week to that and here I am, on a sleek, white catamaran, waiting to fulfil my dream of sailing up the Gordon River through the wilderness of Tassie's south-west forests and, while there, visiting *Sarah Island*, the most notorious of Australia's early penal settlements.

The engines rev, the gangplank is drawn back and we slide out into Macquarie Harbour. I paid extra to ensure myself a window seat but, being the middle of winter, the ship is almost empty and I move up to a raised section in the centre where I can see all around me. Macquarie Harbour is just over 110 square miles of protected water. The only way in and out is through a narrow gap, only 50 feet wide. The harbour is one of the few large bodies of tidal water in the world. With the raging winds of the 'Roaring Forties', and the tide meeting the waves crashing in from the Southern Ocean, the passage into Macquarie Harbour was a terrifying ordeal for those in sailing ships. Worse, there's a sandbank dead across the entrance and so, at spring tide, the depth of water shrinks to just 11 feet. The passage was named, reasonably enough, 'Hell's Gates'. Ships would often wait days for a chance to get in and then many were still lost. Let's hope our skipper knows what he's doing.

A salmon and trout farm sits in the middle of the harbour. The skipper's voice echoes through the speakers. 'It's feeding time. If you look back, you may see a few leaping up for their breakfast.' The engines lull and we bob on the water for a few minutes. No trout or salmon makes the effort. I guess they've learnt they don't need to – probably just lying back with their mouths open. We pass through 'Hell's Gates' easily, do a U-turn in the Southern Ocean and safely return to the quieter waters of the harbour. Morning tea is served and I sit at the bow of the ship, my scarf wrapped tightly against the cutting wind, to wait for my first glimpse of the Gordon River.

In 1978, *the Tasmanian Hydro Electricity Commission* announced its intention to build a dam close to where the Gordon and the environmentally sensitive Franklin River meet. Both areas are *World Heritage* Listed. A protest followed, gradually growing until it involved people from all walks of life and all parts of Australia. In 1983, when Bob Hawke took over from Malcolm Fraser as Prime Minister, he kept his campaign promise to put an end to the plans, although it took a High Court Case against the Tasmanian Government to make it a sure thing. I've seen photos of the Gordon, winding from its source in the Central Highlands, its waters dark and so serene they create a mirror, reflecting the rainforest through which it travels.

'Now,' says the skipper, as we approach a bend, 'get your cameras ready. It's clear today. With a bit of luck, we'll have great reflections.' I do as he says and there it is – a perfect mirror. Dark green, forest-covered mountains, with veils of white cloud drifting across the pale blue of the sky. What is the use of a photo? How can a camera record this beauty? I do, though, to jog my memory when I'm back in my concrete city. The cruise companies have been given permission to create a small landing with an elevated walkway in a loop through the forest. We file off the ship and I enter an ancient realm. Trees soar toward the sky, so tall I can hardly see their tops.

'Huon Pines have been known to live up to three thousand years,' says our guide, 'and there is a known stand who's root base has been in existence for 10,000 years. As you go along you will pass a 2000-year-old pine. That is, it was growing before Christ was born.' I try to get my head around that and give it away. 'It has fallen but its roots are still alive and so saplings are growing from it. I'll leave you to wander. We'll meet back here in half an hour.'

The tree is massive; 2000 years old, unable to stand but still a support to others coming on. Not unlike humans, I guess. Just because our legs can't carry us in our old age doesn't mean we can't still offer support to those coming on though, on the whole, they don't realise it's available till it's too late. I commune with the tree as others glance at it and fade away. The forest is quiet, with only the whisper of ferns and the occasional fluttering of sparse leaves that have been able to survive in the dim light. A half an hour has gone already and I rush back to the ship. We're served lunch as we glide back down the river to the harbour.

***

Until 1856, Tasmania was known as Van Diemen's Land, named by Dutch explorer Abel Tasman, the first European to land on the island, in honour of Anthony Van Diemen, Governor-General of the Dutch East Indies. *Sarah Island*, established in 1822, was set up to detain those convicts that had the cheek to keep escaping from settlements on the mainland. Little remains of the original buildings. Most were made of timber and have rotted away. The brick and stone structures were depleted by souvenir collectors and the forest has reclaimed most of the island.

It's a bleak place. The wind whips off the dark water, the sky is a steely grey and it's cold – freezing. I lean against the wet, moss-covered wall of the ruins of the solitary confinement cells, stone coffins, completely dark with barely enough room to lie down.

'Before the cells were built,' says our guide, one Richard Davey, in a Dryzabone and Akubra, 'prisoners were left on Grummet Island.' He points to a large rock to the north-west. 'No bedding was provided and so they spent the night in the open in their soaked clothes, often still in chains.' I shiver and pull my coat tightly around me. 'Escape from Sarah Island was virtually impossible, due to the treacherous seas that separate the island from the mainland, the wilderness, and the distance from other settlements.'

'Plenty tried,' an elderly man next to me says, quietly. His shock of white hair contrasts, vividly, with a red woollen scarf, tucked tightly into the neck of his well-used duffel coat. He tells me about Matthew Brady, a flamboyant Irishman, transported for forgery. In 1824, he and 14 of his mates stole a boat and sailed it to the Derwent Estuary, before taking to the bush. For nearly two years he led one of the colony's most notorious bushranger gangs.

'He was a folk hero for the settlers,' the man says, 'due to his good manners. Women loved him. And he was a character. When Governor Arthur offered a reward of 25 guineas for his capture, he offered 20 gallons of rum to anyone who could deliver the Governor to him. He was captured, eventually, by the bounty hunter, John Batman, and hanged in 1826 before a crowd of weeping women.'

'What a great story.'

'There's plenty of those.'

'I can understand them risking the forest and the ocean to try and escape. Nothing could have seemed worse than what they had.'

'Or committing murder.'

'Really?'

'A few planned murders so they could get a trip to Hobart and have the distraction of a trial. And then, being hanged was an escape from their nightmare.'

The group starts moving away. Meanwhile, Richard Davey has walked down the bank and is now doing his spiel while standing in the water – in waders, luckily, which is more than the convicts had. His rich, resonant voice floats up to us but I'm having trouble concentrating. Something keeps dragging me away – ghosts, maybe. Pieces of information flicker past me.

'Huon Pines are perfect for ship-building ... a unique oil that makes the wood resistant to fungi.'

'Prisoners spent hours up to their waists in the water ... worked all day on a breakfast of flour and water ... no fruit and vegetables ... disease.' Drips run down my face and I realise it's drizzling. Umbrellas have popped up around me.

'Lash ... solitary confinement ... slavery.'

This was more than punishment – revenge, maybe – or what happens when the normal checks and balances are no longer in place. Macquarie Harbour was so far from the rest of the colony that, in the early days, there was little supervision. Most overseers were ex-convicts and made the most of their first ever experience of power. One monster, Alexander Anderson, designed his lash with double twisted and knotted cords. The permissible maximum at any one time was 100 lashes and he used every one, at every opportunity. To complain was criminal; even an expression of anger added to the punishment.

'Would you like to share our umbrella,' says a plump woman, already sharing it with her plump husband. There's absolutely no way there's room for me but it's thoughtful of her.

'Thanks,' I say, 'I'm fine.' Meanwhile, Richard has returned to dry land and is now standing in what was the bakery, a rivulet running from the rim of his hat.

'The Suffolk oven produced 400 loaves a day. Ergot was added to the bread to cause it to go mouldy. That was to prevent the inmates from stockpiling their food for escape attempts.' Not particularly rational, I would have thought, considering the severe shortage of food at the time and the fact that everything had to be shipped in. 'By 1828, *Sarah Island* was the largest ship-building industry in the colony. It had developed into an industrial village with blacksmiths, tanners, boot makers, medical orderlies, cooks, gardeners and clerks.'

'Did they have a school,' asks a boy of around eight, who has been taking in every word.

'They did,' answers Richard. 'Even here you couldn't get out of going to school.' Quiet laughter ripples around the boy and he blushes. 'Having women and children about had a refining effect on the settlement; that, and the cultivation of healthier food along with religious instruction. A lot of the convicts ended up as skilled tradesmen.'

I wander off to the remains of the courthouse, standing on a small hill, looking out toward the harbour. It seems a strange place for a courthouse, battered by the vicious icy wind that would have ripped through convicts and authority alike. But then the whole setup was strange – an industrial village, literally at the ends of the earth. The women must have wondered where they'd gone wrong to end up here. In fact, everyone sent here must have regarded themselves as prisoners, as they slid further away from civilisation, into such a threateningly alien world. By 1833, it had become too expensive to keep the settlement going and the remaining inmates were transferred to the new prison at Port Arthur.

The drizzling stops and umbrellas are returned to their bags. The group starts moving toward the ship, standing out from the grey and deep green of its surroundings like a beautiful swan. I join them and, in what seems only minutes, we are tying up at the wharf at Strahan.

Chapter 2

'What's with the smog?' I ask the woman behind me in the supermarket queue. I'd had trouble seeing where I was going as I headed down the hill past the Mt. Lyell Copper Mine, nestled in a deep valley on the edge of the old mining town of Queenstown.

'That's not smog, love,' she says, dragging on a cigarette. 'It's fog.'

'Fog,' I say, sceptically. 'So it's nothing to do with the mine?'

'Nah.' She breaks into a rasping smokers' cough. 'Nothin' wrong with the mine. It's just fog.'

I'm not convinced. Around 10.15am, though, it lifts. By 10.30 it's gone. The wide main street is dominated by several enormous hotels, built during the establishment of the mine in the late 1800s. Verandas, bordered by balustrades of iron lacework and timber, jut from iron roofs, to shelter the pavement and shops below. I look up toward the glowering hills that fill the space at the other end. This could be a movie set – the 'Wild West', except Australian. Exchange a few cars for horses and it would be ready. Looking at some of the locals, they wouldn't need to go far for extras.

I've often been told I have to see the dead hills on the way out of town, all vegetation having been killed off years before by the felling of trees to burn in the mine smelters and the sulphur fumes from the smelters themselves. I look up at the narrow road hanging from the side of the cliffs, curving and climbing its way into the distance, and cringe. I've been giving myself challenges for a while in an attempt to cure my fear of heights. It hasn't worked yet, though, and there's no other way out of town, so I grit my teeth, quote some clichéd affirmation about confidence in my abilities and press the accelerator.

I hug the cliff, my hands glued to the steering wheel, pouring with sweat. I can't look around me. If I do I'll drive off the edge – I know I will; there's nothing to stop me. A caravan glides toward me from the opposite direction. I can't believe this road is wide enough for the two of us and I wait for the thump that will knock me into the valley below. It passes without incident, though I'm not sure how close it came because I think I had my eyes shut. Five kilometres later, my muscles screaming with tension, I enter the forest on the other side of town. I'll have to buy a postcard in Hobart to see what I missed out on.

I navigate mile after mile of mountainous corners. My daughter's voice echoes in my head. *You are in the wild west, Mum.* If only I'd heard that earlier, I would have come from the other direction and left this challenging section of the trip till last when I'd had more practice on the roads. I *had* checked everything, though. I researched. I sat in the bath for hours staring at maps and tourist guides. This terrain is *not* on the maps. At least I'm on the cliff side and, thinking about it, I couldn't have come from the other direction. My fear of heights would have become a self-fulfilling prophecy. I would have disappeared over the edge to become permanently 'World Heritage' listed.

The scent of the forest wafts through the open window and I start calming down. There's no rush, after all. I don't have to be in Hobart till tomorrow. I can take this slowly and enjoy what I'm doing. The huge trees fill every part of my landscape and my situation dawns on me. I am in one of the most beautiful places in the world. This is what I came for. I relax back into a sea of green.

***

A bird, a large, cheeky creature with mottled black and white stripes down its back, red feet and a viciously long beak, is trying to steal a crust from my sandwich bag. He scares me a bit, with his aggressive manner. I swear he would take my finger if it had food attached. I've arrived at the bottom end of Lake St. Clair in Cradle Valley National Park. The icy breeze creeps up my leg and I pull my sock up further. I could grab the air, pick up a piece of it, it's so crisp and white. 'Actually, it hasn't been too bad lately,' the park ranger says to me when I complain, just a little, about the cold. Is she being smug or do they just get used it?

A path curves away out of sight and so I pack my thermos and esky back in the car, wrap my scarf around my neck and follow it. The picture, as I round the corner, is straight out of the English children's books I grew up with. Moss is everywhere, covering the ground, fallen branches, tree trunks, everything that has stayed still. Little grows in the dim light on the forest floor. A wallaby scratches in the dead leaves, oblivious to me. Trees zoom toward the light.

The sound of water draws me to a bridge over, not a creek, a sweet gentle thing but a river, energetic and vibrant, pouring down an incline, crashing over rocks and stones, earth and branches, everything in its path, carving its way through its territory. It's hard for me to immediately take in the beauty of this scene; my mind argues that it can't be real. A young couple strolls past, hand in hand, and I nod.

'Have you by any chance seen any pandani?' the young woman asks. I don't know what pandani is.

'Don't think so, sorry.'

'We were hoping to see some,' says her partner. They hang over the railing, arms around each other, gazing into the water.

I drag myself away and follow the path again, arriving at a small beach in a bay area, looking out across the expanse of Lake St. Clair. Sitting on a rock I watch the tiny waves lap the sand. A wren picks at something near my feet and I stay perfectly still, not wanting to disturb it. A light plane whirrs far above my head and fades into nothing. Voices pass on the pathway and drift away. A movement at the side of me catches my attention and I watch an echidna ease itself from under a log and wobble its way along the sand and back into the undergrowth. Though I can hear a gentle twittering of birds, there's a stillness and a feeling of safety, as if the trees are guarding me. The trees are safe too, so far, protected by *World Heritage* Listing. Their leaves rustle far above me. A small grey and pink bird, a robin, I think, lands next to me, flicks its tail then takes off again. Everything here knows its place: the animals, the birds, the trees and moss, water and rocks – and me.

***

'Can I help you with something?' says a man, coming out of the gloom toward me.

'I'm looking for a caravan park. Is this Tarraleah? There's supposed to be a caravan park.'

'There was. It's gone.'

The sign to Tarraleah, halfway between Strahan and Hobart, had directed me onto an unsealed road that gradually turned into a track that seemed to be heading nowhere. As I was deciding to turn back, the forest disappeared behind me and I am now surrounded by paddocks, a huge hydro-electricity pipeline and strange-looking, half-completed buildings. It's almost dark and I have nowhere to stay for the night. *Book somewhere between Strahan and Hobart*, my daughter had said. *I'll be right*, I answered, *it's winter. It'll be easy to get in somewhere.* She looked worried.

'You can try at the office.'

'Where's that?' I ask, trying to make out anything looking like an office.

'Go back down this road and you'll come to it.'

I backtrack to where light is eking through a heavy glass door. Two tradesmen are unravelling coils of electricity cables. Sheets of plaster sit against the walls and nails and screws litter the floor. Panic must be showing in my face because they stop and stare at me.

'I need some help.'

'Over there,' one of them says, pointing to a woman sitting at a desk.

'Excuse me,' I call, too loudly. She looks up in surprise. 'The *Royal Automobile Club of Victoria* guide said there's a caravan park here.'

'No, not any more. We're building a resort. Won't be ready for months, though.'

'I've got nowhere to stay. Is there anywhere else around?' She stands up and comes across to me.

'No, not around here.' Again, I'm trapped in the mountains, in the dark, exhausted. 'You could go back to *Bronte Park*. I could ring them for you if you like.' *Bronte Park* is the resort outside of Lake St. Clair that I chose to bypass because of the caravan park at Tarraleah.

'How far is it?'

'About half an hour.' I consider the trek back on the valley side of the road in the dark, and know I'm too tired to handle it.

'There's a caravan park at Hamilton. I'll head for that.' She looks anxious.

'You sure?'

'Yes.'

'Okay,' she says. 'Good luck.'

Nothing is open after six o'clock in the wild west of Tasmania. Maybe Tasmanians hibernate in winter, go into caves, perhaps, and emerge three months later. Hamilton is in darkness; both caravan parks are closed. All of the tourist information suggested I do the detour to the 'historic village' of Hamilton. Hamilton was going to bail me out. I'm not sure how long my petrol will last. I haven't seen a service station since Queenstown.

I have two options: to keep going or try for a 'Bed and Breakfast', if I can find one. The 'historic village' of Hamilton is sure to have some, at around $140 a night. Or I could sleep in the car. 'B&B', continue or sleep in the car?

The lights of New Norfolk glow and the petrol tank is on empty. A sign flashes on the white wall of an old hotel in Montague Street. *Vacancy $30.* $30? For the whole night? I'll *do* it. The bistro is large, warmed by a huge log fire. I stand at the counter, wondering why I'm not being spoken to. It's a common experience of mine, a feeling that I'm not really there with the other humans in the room, cut off somehow, as if I can't be seen. I look desperately around me.

'You want something?' says a man, getting up from the middle of a family group and coming across to me.

'I need a room.' He looks flustered. Why does he look flustered? Didn't the sign say *Vacancy*?

'Right,' he says, 'it's $30.'

'I've come from Strahan and I couldn't find anywhere to stay and I've driven for hours in the dark and I thought I might have run out of petrol ...' I'm gabbling.

'Come over to the bar,' he says, walking away.

I sit with my vodka and orange in front of the fire and wait for a plate of what's left of the bistro food. The Bush Inn has an amazing history. Opened by Ann Bridger in 1825, it holds the title of Australia's oldest continuously licensed hotel. Among its claims to fame is the visit of Dame Nellie Melba in 1924 when she sang, *Scenes That Are Brightest.* The song was from the opera, *Maritana,* written by William Vincent Wallace in 1838, while inspired by the rural scene from the hotel veranda. History was made at the hotel on June 29th, 1932, when *Maritana* was produced and broadcast over the national radio network for the first time, through station *7ZL* Hobart. Two records from the broadcast are mounted over the fireplace.

Australia's first trunk call was made between Hobart and the *Bush Inn*. Its proprietor, Octavius Blockley, received the call from the Hobart Post Office on 1st December, 1888. The first call to London was also made from here on February 1, 1939. The phone sits in a glass case in the foyer beside, strangely, a christening font. The font has been here since 1835, when Methodist preachers from the *Melville Street Chapel* in Hobart, used the inn as a chapel, preaching to their congregation in the old 'tap room'. Very convenient if you fancy a quiet drink after Sunday service. On 17th February 1989, the hotel was officially classified by the *National Trust*.

The oldness of the surroundings nurtures and comforts me. I finish my meal and wandering back through the dimly lit, ragged, common room, I meet a resident of the hotel, a man in his 40s, who tells me the problems he has in keeping contact with his son. I'm happy to listen, letting the everyday conversation bring me back to earth. The shower is cold but the bed is comfortable and the breakfast in front of the fire, delicious. This is where I'll stay next time around. I stop off to fill up on petrol and head back along the highway to Mt. Field National Park and Russell Falls.

***

'Gosh, you must love working here,' I say to the man, as he passes my coffee across the counter. He looks at me vaguely for a moment and I feel a need to elaborate. The cafeteria is plonked in the middle of the Mt. Field National Park rainforest. I wave my hand towards the windows. 'It's stunning, isn't it?'

'Ah, yes,' he says, and turns away. Maybe you'd get used to it if you worked in it all day, though I don't think I would ever become blasé towards this. Rejuvenated by my coffee, I follow the signs directing me along a pathway to Russell Falls. The pale white light of the sky leaks through a world of every shade of green. The waterfall appears from the forest, high above me. It's partly covered by ferns and trees and so I follow the sign pointing me to the top for a better look. The pathway is wet, muddy and slippery. As it rises it becomes narrower and narrower. On one side of me is a sheer drop and on the other, a sheer, muddy cliff.

This can't be the tourist walk to Russell Falls, surely. There's no-one else here. Have I taken a wrong turn? I ease myself around to the cliff and stand, face and hands attached looking, no doubt, a bit like a gecko on a summer's night, and contemplate my situation. My mind knows I'm not in danger but my body has a totally different opinion. One of the difficulties of the fear of heights phobia, is that you freeze. You can't move to get yourself out of the situation. If there was a railing to hold onto I would be fine but no-one has thought it necessary to provide one.

Still, I can't stand here all day and it will be extremely embarrassing if someone comes up behind me. There's no way I can continue upwards, not knowing where the path is leading. I'll have to go back. With my hands attached to the cliff, displaying myself as the world's most neurotic woman, I descend, step by step, back to the safety of the forest floor, checking the sign on the way. It *is* the tourist path to the top of Russell Falls and there *isn't* mention of the pathway becoming suitable only for mountain goats.

Back in New Norfolk, I park beside the river and wander along its bank. The town was the third oldest planned settlement, after Hobart and Launceston. Starting in 1807, inhabitants of the *Norfolk Island Penal Colony* were encouraged to come to Van Diemen's Land to help populate the areas around the Derwent River. Thirty per cent of them came to New Norfolk.

Being transported was not necessarily the worst thing that could happen, especially for someone with entrepreneurial gifts. Denis McCarty was an Irish political prisoner, transported to New South Wales in 1803. McCarty quickly converted from convict to police constable and in 1808, was appointed to New Norfolk. He married Mary Wainwright, who was born on Norfolk Island, the daughter of First Fleeter, Hester Wainwright. By 1811, he was entertaining Governor Macquarie at his home.

In 1812, he was granted 50 acres of land for farming, and not long after that, he won the construction contract to build the road from Hobart Town to New Norfolk. Exploring was also a passion and he sailed ships from Macquarie Harbour to Kangaroo Island, and as far north as Port Jackson. A large boulder with a plaque stands on the bank of the river, as a monument to him.

The settlement grew and in 1846 the first hop plants were brought from Maria Island. This began a thriving industry and accounts for the odd-looking oast houses along the way here, used for drying and processing hops before they were sent to the local breweries. It's a pretty town surrounded by undulating hills, valleys and streams, with the Derwent River running through the centre – a perfect place to relax before braving the metropolis of Hobart.

Chapter 3

'God, things are hard to find in this place!'
'Is that right?' says the woman. I've eventually found the tourist park on the other side of the river on the outskirts of Hobart. 'I followed the directions and kept ending up in a housing estate. There's something wrong with the road signs.'

'Well, you're here now,' she says, soothingly. 'You can relax.' Now, if the ogre in Strahan had said that to me, I'd have been over my stress in a shot. She fills me in on the facilities of the park and the times of buses into the city.

'We've given you Number 12. It's one of our nicest. Park beside the door and if there's anything else we can help you with, just ask.'

I'm inordinately pleased that someone is treating me like a human being. It's all you need, really, after a day on the road. You can do the rest yourself. My daughter must have told them about my trip to Tassie being a birthday gift. A small bottle of champagne sits on the table with chocolates and a message wishing me happy birthday. I realise, when I stop moving, how tired I am. I sit for half an hour, my champagne in a glass from the kitchen cupboard, and stare through the screen door to the next cabin. Draining the glass I fill it again. The bottle is empty already – disappointing. Exhausted, I lie on the bed and fall asleep.

***

You have to go to the Salamanca Market, my daughter had said, *but it's only there on Saturdays.* It's eight degrees, grey and drizzling, as I raise my umbrella and step off the bus. I start with a coffee in a pleasant Italian cafe then, my trusty city map in my hand, head toward the dock area and Salamanca Place.

'I've just come from there,' I say to a man in a stall filled with stunning photos of the west coast and Queenstown. 'Coming out through the hills I couldn't look. I thought I was going to die.'

'Yeah?' says a man next to me. 'I went in from the other direction – *with* a caravan.'

'Oh, my God.'

'Never again,' he says. '*Never again.*'

I'm ridiculously relieved to hear that someone else found it difficult. There are others with my neurosis, it seems. It *is* a neurosis, I guess. After all, why would you drive off the road – or fall off a cliff? Why, if you can drive on a flat surface, can't you drive just as safely on a mountain? I keep pushing, though. One day I'll win.

I'm disappointed in the market. Maybe on a warm, sunny day I would enjoy it more. It seems quite touristy to me; a lot of cheap products from Asia that I could get anywhere. I find a nice necklace, though, from Peru - $20. I'm guessing, from the price, the stones aren't precious.

***

'You can't go in today,' the woman says to me, 'there's a rehearsal on.'

'Never mind, I just thought I'd ask.'

Dubbed by Noel Coward as 'a dream of a theatre', the *Theatre Royal* opened in 1837 and is Australia's oldest working theatre. It was designed by Peter Degraves, founder of Tasmania's famous *Cascade Brewery*, amid the public houses, brothels, factories and workers' cottages of Wapping. Its entertainment ranged from music hall to cock fights, even helping to quench the thirst of patrons at *The Shades*, a seedy tavern that operated beneath the theatre, with its own entrance door into the pit. It's rumoured that during intervals, drunken prostitutes could be seen bounding across the seats to get to the conveniences, much to the chagrin of the gentry in the boxes. It survived a fire and was saved from demolition several times, most notably in the late 1940s, when Sir Laurence Olivier jumped to its defence. It's recently been renovated and being an amateur 'theatric' from way back, I was hoping to have a look around. She picks up on my disappointment.

'Well, maybe just for a minute. It's a school production and they're opening tonight so they mustn't be disturbed in any way. We can look in but you *mustn't* speak.'

I promise not to say a word. The theatre is round, its seats covered in burgundy velvet and its balconies elaborately ornamented in gold and silver. A giant dome oversees the stalls, dropping a crystal chandelier from its centre. I yearn to go backstage, to stand in the same spot as Laurence Olivier and Vivien Leigh in 1948, as they awaited their cues in *The School for Scandal*.

'I've done a lot of revue myself,' I've completely forgotten my promise not to talk, 'so I wanted to have a look at *this* theatre.' My voice always gets louder when I'm excited. 'It's *so* famous.' She pushes her hand into my back and I grab another look before she hurries me out.

'Thanks so much for that,' I say, 'it's gorgeous.' I'm 'sucking up' to make up for talking loudly, but it works.

'Yes,' she says. 'We had Jackie Weaver and Barry Otto a couple of months ago and they were thrilled to be performing here. They said it's their favourite theatre.' I believe her. She rushes away.

***

'I'm not there yet. Just wait a minute.'

'Sorry.'

He's irritated with me for asking questions; I'm interfering with his spiel. I'm a tour group of one, being guided around the *Penitentiary Chapel and Courthouse*. The guide is pedantic about covering all the information in perfect order but he's very knowledgeable and I'm very interested, so I allow myself to be led through underground passages, solitary confinement cells and the execution yard. Developers wanted to wipe the lot off the map to make way for modern buildings but the city's judges insisted that it be saved and both courthouses remained in use until 1983. The site is now a *National Trust* Property.

'The site was designed by John Lee Archer,' he continues, 'the Government Civil Engineer and Architect.

By 1829, *St. David's Church* was becoming so overcrowded that a second Anglican church was needed for the free inhabitants to worship in comfort. A place of religious instruction was also needed for the increasing numbers of convicts. That's why it was built opposite the Prisoners' Barracks in Brisbane Street. The Barracks housed convicts taken out on daily work parties for road and building construction.'

'Makes sense.'

'Did you know that by 1830 there were 10,000 convicts in Van Diemen's Land?'

'Gosh, no, I didn't.'

Prisoners and free settlers attended services in the chapel together, examining each other from opposite wings. This caused much interest between the daughters of the local families and the convicts until the chaplain, Rev. Philip Palmer, spoilt the fun by installing a screen, thereby cutting the convicts off from the rest of the congregation. In 1847, the prison barracks Superintendant, James Boyd, reported that "it is most gratifying to me in being able to state that the convicts show the utmost attention and propriety of demeanour (sic) during Divine Service and apparently feel interested in the very excellent discourses which are delivered to them."

Linus W. Miller, a 22-year-old Canadian lawyer, transported after becoming involved in the 1838 Canadian rebellion, observed: "On looking about me, I could not discover more than twelve, among twelve hundred prisoners, who appeared to be taking any notice of the service. Some were spinning yarns, some playing at pitch and toss, some gambling with cards; several were crawling about under the benches selling candy, tobacco, &c., and one fellow carried a bottle of rum which he was serving out in small quantities to those who had an English sixpence to give for a small wine glass full."

We stand in front of a hole in the floor. Thirty-six solitary confinement cells were placed beneath the floor of the chapel and this is one of them.

'They had no light or ventilation,' my guide says, 'and varied in height to support the inclined floors above them. The entrances to the smallest cells were only 70 centimetres high and so they named them, the 'Dust Hole'. They were declared inhuman in 1847 and sealed up.'

'A bit late for most of the convicts.'

'Yes, when you consider the worst crime for some of them was returning home drunk from their daily work party.' It's a horrifying thought, men lying entombed while the service went on above them. 'Would you like to test one of the cells?' he says, smiling sweetly. I smile sweetly back at him and move on, wondering at the cruelty of the times that accepted this as normal.

'In 1859, the nave and eastern transept of the chapel were converted into two Supreme Criminal Courts, joined by an underground passageway, to allow easy access for prisoners. The western transept remained to become a gaol chapel, with an execution yard and gallows.' Conviction, prayer and execution – all in the one spot. Very organised.

The first execution took place on 18th August, 1857. The *Hobart Town Mercury* reported the next day that "the unhappy man seemed perfectly resigned to his fate." Margaret Coghlin was the only woman executed here, accused of killing her husband. She was discovered by a policeman hanging from her window calling, 'Oh Lord, bless me, he's come home and cut his throat.' She went to the gallows with her eyes bandaged and trembling so much she had to be supported. She left a confession, blaming 'strong drink' for her crime. The noose hangs from a low ceiling in a covered-in section of the execution yard.

'It's a wonderful place, history-wise,' I say, as we arrive at the door to the outside world.

'Yes, it's the real thing alright.' He waves me off and closes the door. It must be a strange place to spend your days, in dark passages, grim, claustrophobic cells and, I'm quite sure, the odd ghost.

It's 3pm and I thought I might wait around and catch a play at one of the theatres, but walking up and down the hills is taking its toll on me. Tasmania seems to be one big mountain range. I cross the road and catch the bus back.

Chapter 4

'What do you think of it?' the man asks, quietly, in the gift shop of the *Old Hobart Town Model Village* in Richmond.

'It's fabulous.' With a good picture of the layout of Hobart's city centre in my mind, from my explorations yesterday, I'm able to appreciate, even more, this perfect model of how it was in the beginning. I'm a total sucker for miniatures and so I check every building, every little figure, the river, horses and carts, kangaroos, washing on the line, even the convict on the scaffold. 'Who did it all?'

'I did.'

'Really? How long did it take you?'

'Three years. It has to be updated all the time, though. Bits get worn – and damaged.'

He looks irritable and I interpret that as having been caused by the two unruly children that had just passed through. I suppose you would spend a lot of your time anxious when years of hard work could be wrecked by one ignorant family. His creation is now one of the main tourist attractions of the area. I wish him well.

Richmond is on the Coal River and was one of the first areas to be settled, not long after the colony was established in 1803. It was used as a crossing point for people travelling by land to the Tasman and Freycinet peninsulas. About the same time, Lieutenant-Governor Arthur chose the area as a police district and the gaol, the court house, the barracks and the watch house were erected. The number of inns increased, businesses were established and trade between Hobart and Richmond flourished.

In 1872, to cut down on travel times, a causeway was opened from Orielton Lagoon to Sorell, by-passing Richmond. Around the same time, the Launceston to Hobart railway was extended through Campania to the north-west, and for the next 100 years the town became a quiet, rural backwater. In the 1970's, the significance of its history was recognised, and the town is now one of the most important tourist destinations in the State.

I choose a delightful tearoom, one of many set up in heritage homes along the main road, to shout myself a morning coffee and scones. Scones are risky I always think. Often they're dry and heavy and you never get enough butter to soften them up. But I'm on an adventure and so I take another risk. They *are* pretty heavy but the girl is happy to get me more butter and the coffee goes down well. I sit for a while in the comforting cheerfulness of the yellow room and let the sunshine from the window waft through me.

Richmond Gaol is the oldest intact gaol in Australia. Pre-dating Port Arthur by five years, it was a cornerstone of the convict system created by Governor Arthur. Floggings were frequent, though a Magistrate could only order a maximum of 36 lashes without a doctor being present. Very considerate. Each of the 12 solitary confinement cells measured 2.13 metres by 1 metre, and prisoners were left there for days at a time. Overcrowding was a constant complaint. Along with prisoners awaiting trial and the convicts, chained road gangs were brought in to be housed at night. Men slept in passages, solitary cells, anywhere they could find a spot. I can only imagine how cold it would be lying on these stone floors.

Inmates engraved their names in the shutters. Thomas Lake carved his name along with his home village, Writtle, in the County of Essex. As a 20-year-old, he was transported for highway robbery. After arriving, he was sent to Richmond Gaol for 'burglarously' entering a house. In1852, his 'ticket of leave' was revoked when he was caught boarding the *Providence* at Hobart, intending to escape. This landed him an extra four and a half years in the Pittwater Quarry Gang. Thomas was either desperately homesick or incredibly dumb. He received his free pardon at last in August, 1858.

Robert Charles was a 15-year-old Scottish lad, transported in 1837 for being 'at thief for years'. After a term at Port Arthur he received his 'ticket of leave' but was locked up in Richmond Gaol for stealing three sheep from Lawrence Cotham, Licensee of the *Richmond Hotel*. His brother, just a year older, was convicted of the same crime. The boys were regularly charged with the same offences. They must have been inseparable.

The Cookhouse was added in 1835, along with accommodation and solitary confinement cells for women. Most of the women at Richmond were there for minor offences such as disorderly conduct or disobedience of orders. Others were simply 'returned to Government' from assignment, a system under which free settlers were allocated convict labourers in return for feeding, clothing and housing them.

The sexism of English society was brought to Australia with the ships and amplified by penal conditions. A woman needed to be particularly strong to survive the stereotypes of 'whorishness' and 'worthlessness' attributed to her. One Scottish settler, Peter Murdoch, who owned more than six thousand acres, remarked "they are generally so bad that the settlers have no heart to treat them well." On the other hand, James Mitchell, a free settler on Norfolk Island, wrote, "Surely no common mortal could demand treatment so brutal. Heaven give their weary footsteps, their aching hearts to a better place of rest, for here there is none." One of the women has hung around, it seems, maybe waiting for a chance to get her own back. Sightings of a ghost in a long, pink dress were first reported in 1850 and locals have heard eerie footsteps in the courtyard at night.

I first learnt about Richmond Bridge at primary school and have been waiting to visit it ever since. Convict built, it came to represent, for me, the history of white settlement in this country. Completed in 1823, it is Australia's oldest bridge still in use and is in its original condition. I gaze across at its lovely sandstone arches. Swans glide along the river and ducks squabble over bits of bread thrown by a family of children picnicking on the grass. The cold has eased, the sky is blue and the sun is shining. I would like to stay in this beautiful little town for days but I'm aiming to explore as much as I can of the east coast and the caves at Mole Creek before catching the ferry back home in five days time.

***

'I was looking for somewhere for a couple of nights,' I say to the young woman in the peaked cap at the Swansea Holiday Park. 'How much are the cabins?'

'$80.'

'$80 ... right.' The weather has taken a turn for the worse, the temperature has dropped about 10° since I left Richmond and the sky is a dark grey, threatening at least heavy rain if not a storm.

'What about a caravan?'

'Vans are $50.' I've been careful but still my monetary situation is beginning to look as dire as the weather. She waits patiently while I consider. $80 for an en suite or $50 to brave the elements, possibly in the middle of the night, at the amenities block. I look around. The park seems empty; it's the middle of winter, there are no school holidays to fill it with families. What's to stop her filling a cabin with me – at a cheaper price? That would be a sensible business decision. She reads my mind.

'I'll tell you what. We've just cleaned a little studio cabin. You can have that for $50.' She's pretty pleased with herself for the offering and I'm pretty pleased with her, too. The cabin is perfect, just big enough for one person, and wraps around me like a cocoon. It's freezing, but I want to explore before the weather takes over completely. Wrapped in several layers, I wind my way between caravans to a small gate, onto a pathway between coastal grasses and onto the beach. A huge bay opens up before me, headlands stretching away to my right and left. Across the centre, where I would have expected to see ocean, is a long strip of deep purple mountains. It takes me a minute to get my breath back and realise where I am. This is Great Oyster Bay and the mountains are the Freycinet Peninsula.

I push against the vicious wind, along the sand to the cape of Waterloo Point and follow an easy incline up *Loontitetermairrelorner Walking Track*, a pathway the locals organised, to protect wildlife and the cultural and natural values of the area. It's a little more sheltered here and I sit for a while, looking out over the bay as the sky deepens from its dark grey to almost black. The rain starts and, for today, I realise I'll have to give in and go back to my cocoon.

***

The early morning sun sprays the clouds as I shut the little gate behind me and trudge down the path, saturated from the rain during the night. The purple contours of the Freycinet stand out against the mauve-tinged, grey sky. The wind has dropped and, except for the wet sand sucking at my runners so that I feel like I'm ploughing through freshly poured cement, it's an easy walk to Waterloo Point. A sign stands close to the track:

"The vessel all this time kept turning on her side more and more and the sea washing right over us, the children then became very weak and we kept hold of them as long as we could with one hand being obliged to hold on ourselves with the other, until the sea washed them away from the different persons who had hold of them." Thomas Large. Inquest 2413, 9th November 1850, Archives Office of Tasmania.

In 1850, Thomas Large, a publican, living with his wife, Mary Ann and their six children at the Swansea Inn, had plans to establish a brewery in town. He travelled to Hobart to collect the necessary equipment and supplies, before being joined by the family for a holiday. On the return journey, the cutter, *Resolution,* was caught in high winds and wrecked. All of the children, aged between 12 and two, were lost. It's not known how Mrs. Large escaped but Mr. Large was unconscious for hours after having been thrown on shore by the surf. All of the bodies except that of eight-year-old William, were recovered, and are buried in the cemetery overlooking the bay. The parents, grief-stricken, returned to Hobart to stay.

Fresh flowers sit at the foot of the gravestone. The script reads:

To the memory of Elizabeth, Aged 12 years, Edmund, Aged 10 years, William, Aged 8 years, Hannah, Aged 6 years, George, Aged 4 years, Frances, Aged 2 years. The above were the Children of Thomas and Mary Ann Large, who were unfortunately drowned at the time of the wreck of the Cutter Resolution at Great Swan Port, on the 5th of Nov 1850.

> *Weep not for us but be content,*
> *We was not yours but only lent,*
> *Wipe of those tears and weep no more,*
> *We are not lost but gone before,*
> *We was not yours but Christ's alone,*
> *He loved us best and called us home.*

I wonder if, in those days, they took sailing off into the wild blue yonder in a ship without an engine, in their stride, or if they quietly worried about arriving in one piece. They had little choice if they wanted to go any distance in this wild land, where roads were often just muddy tracks. I guess you can put anything out of your mind if you need to. After all, we go 30,000 feet in the air, often without giving it a thought.

The *Loontitetermairrelehorner Track* takes me round the headland into town. A few locals scurry in and out of shops, their heads down, anxious to get back to the warmth of their homes. Before long I realise they have the right idea. I grab a packet of pasta from the supermarket and head back, just beating the rain, and spend the afternoon wrapped up in front of the heater with a book.

***

I'm disappointed the young woman in the peaked cap isn't around as I enter the office to return the key. I want to thank her for my hiatus in this beautiful spot in this pretty town.

'How was the cabin?' says a woman, her mother maybe, or a local filling in.

'Perfect.'

'I cleaned it myself ... went through it like a steam train.'

'Perfect,' I repeat. She glows. I take a side street down to Waterloo Point for a last look and see a sign I missed yesterday, taken up with the tragedy of the ship-wrecked children: *Erected by the Tasmanian Society to commemorate the exploration and charting of this coast by NICHOLAS BAUDIN French Navigator February 1802.*

Baudin and English explorer, Matthew Flinders, were sent by their respective governments to chart and explore the southern coast of Australia. They crossed paths at Encounter Bay on the east coast of South Australia, in April, 1802. Hence, many places originally had both French and English names. Flinders was scrupulous in honouring prior discoveries and so the Freycinet is named after Louis de Freycinet, Baudin's cartographer. Baudin died on his way home in 1803 and his charts were completed by Freycinet, who eventually restored many of Flinders' original names. It was a peaceful agreement between two countries that were otherwise endlessly at loggerheads with each other.

***

The Freycinet Peninsula is one of the places you have to do. That's what *Tourism Tasmania* tells us, anyway, and I'm sick of just looking at photos of Wineglass Bay. I want to see it for myself. I flash my *National Parks* card at the girl behind the counter.

'The lookout for Wineglass Bay. Is it a hard walk?' She shakes her head. 'So it's not difficult, then?'

'No, it's okay.'

She obviously hasn't done it – or being still a lithe teenager, wouldn't have noticed the incline if she had. Middle-aged couples are draped variously along the track, faces purple and hearts pounding.

'The girl told me this was going to be easy,' I say to a rotund man, who's going so slowly, even I pass him. He mumbles something in reply and forges onwards. It's at this moment that the sun comes out, for once not helping my situation but making me even hotter. I finally reach the lookout and join a grumpy-looking woman and her husband and their children.

'Look, Sean,' the father says to an eight-year-old. 'Look at the view.' Sean ignores him. 'Will, come and look.'

'I can't see,' says Will, without moving.

'Emily.' He points across toward a sliver of Wineglass Bay. A 12-year-old girl materialises and squeezes up against him.

'Can we go?' whines Sean.

'I'm tired,' carps William. Emily and her father exchange a look. The mother starts moving away and the boys suddenly get their energy back and pound down the steps. I must admit, I'm a little disappointed myself. No, I'm very disappointed. The sliver of Wineglass Bay is just that – a sliver. Obviously, this is not where the photos are taken from. Maybe I took the wrong track, read the wrong sign. It's a regular failing of mine. The trek back down gives me a chance to look around me. The Peninsula is, effectively, two massive, eroded blocks of granite – the Hazards and Mt. Graham – joined by a sand isthmus. It seems impossible that anything could erode these majestic, apparently impenetrable, giants. Halfway down, I stop and rest against a massive rock, vacated by a couple heading upwards. The rain and freezing wind of yesterday is gone and the dark stone glitters in the sun.

***

Swansea is just one of many gorgeous little fishing towns sprinkled along the east coast and, even though I'm now tired and it's late afternoon, I have to discipline myself to keep moving. If I stop at every one I won't reach my accommodation at St. Helen's before midnight. It's raining again, as I negotiate a steep, narrow, winding road in the dark, looking for St. Helen's Holiday Park. It seems an odd site for it – I was expecting it to be at the beach – and just as I decide to find somewhere to turn around and go back, it appears. All I want to do is wrap myself up in my cabin and hibernate, but I promised myself a decent meal in a bistro – you can only go so long without vegetables. I stick my head out the door. The rain is now in sheets, the wind blasts through me and I decide one more day without vegetables is not going to kill me. Riffling through my bags I discover a small tin of baked beans I'd forgotten was there. Beans are good for you, aren't they?

***

St. Helens was originally a whaling town, first settled in 1830. It would have remained quiet and inconsequential if not for the discovery of tin in 1874, in the mountains of the *Blue Tiers*. Within three years, mines were established at Branxholm, Weldborough, Bradshaw's Creek and, the largest of them all, the Briseis Tin Mine at Derby. The north-east generated a large proportion of the island's wealth for the next century. The town is now Tasmania's busiest fishing port, with a large fleet of fishing boats in Georges Bay. It's vibrant-looking, even in the middle of winter – very touristy. Every second building seems to be a motel or holiday apartment block.

The houses and cottages on the outskirts fade behind me and forest and mist close around. Fine rain colours everything grey and I would rather be spending the morning in front of a log fire with a coffee, surrounded by cheerful company, than peering through the windscreen of this car. The forest gives way to lush paddocks and a sign points along a side road to *Pyengana Dairy Company and Cafe.* This could be my warmth and cheerful company.

No such luck. I'm the only customer and, with the wooden floors, the room is yet to warm up. I gaze out toward the cows, undisturbed by the rain and cold, and to the vague outline of mountains in the distance, and return to the winters of my childhood, trying to stay warm in the dairy region of Victoria's Gippsland. An SUV pulls into the car park and two children tumble out. They glance at me as they enter and rush to a table in the centre of the room.

'Can we sit here, Daddy?' yells the six-year-old boy. 'Can we? Can we sit here?'

'Can we sit here, Daddy,' mimics his little sister. The mother nods and after a short squabble over a chair, the boy gives in and they settle themselves down.

'I want a *Coke*. Can I have a *Coke*?'

'Can I have a *Coke*?' says the girl.

'No, you're not having *Coke*, it's bad for you.'

'It's bad for you,' says the girl to her brother. The parents order two hot chocolates, a cappuccino and a skinny decaf latte, and join the children at the table. They natter together while the children kick their legs, impatiently.

'When's it coming?' says the boy. The girl heaves a great sigh, jumps up from her chair and runs to the window.

'Look, Mummy,' she calls, 'a cow ... Mummy, there's a big cow ... Mummy.'

'Jessica,' says the mother, 'come back to the table.'

'Mummy, a big cow.' She taps her fingers sharply on the window. I'm on the verge of answering her myself when the mother says, again, 'Jessica, come back to the table.'

'Jessica,' says the father. Jessica drops her hand and her head and hurries back. No doubt, when she's a teenager, not too far in the future, they'll complain she never tells them anything. She turns to her brother and they also natter together. I finish my coffee and leave them to their family stuff.

***

Someone toots me angrily. I've done something wrong but I have no idea what it is. It's the first time I've been anywhere near Launceston, let alone in late afternoon traffic when the city workers are heading home. I guess he's one of them but I've had a long day, too, so we're all in the same boat. I'm not at all sure I'm going in the right direction, or even know where I am. There's no chance of checking at this moment so I sit in the middle lane and get carried along in the stream. It divides and I find myself, after only one failed attempt, following a sign to the Hadspen Holiday Park.

'$90,' the woman says.

'$90? I'm on my own. Is that all you've got?'

'That's for the standard cabin,' she says.

It's a very nice cabin but I'm paying for six berths. Surely it's time singles, and couples for that matter, were given consideration. I guess holiday parks *are* made for families – and we singles and couples *can* always find a hotel room. But I like them; they give me access to a kitchen and the freedom of cooking my own meals instead of having to wait around for someone else to do it for me. If *I* ran a holiday park, I would have a couple of small cabins tucked away for those, like myself, who wanted to pop in at the last moment. That's not much to ask, surely.

Chapter 5

One of my daughter's strong recommendations was the caves at Mole Creek. 'You're too late for the current tour of *Marakoopa*,' says the park ranger, 'but you'll catch *King Solomons* if you go now.'

'That's back in the direction I came from?'

'Go back down to the main road and turn left. Follow that for 12 kilometres. When that's finished, come back here and you'll be in time for the next tour of *Marakoopa*.'

'Is it worth doing both, do you think?'

'They *are* quite different. *Marakoopa* is a river cave and has the glow worms but my favourite is *King Solomons*. It's *so* beautiful. I would definitely recommend both.' I set off into 12 kilometres of thick rainforest. Just as I'm wondering if I'm lost and maybe heading into some *World Heritage* Listed wilderness, the forest opens out to an almost empty car park. An extra pair of socks and an added windcheater, gloves and a scarf allow me to leave the warmth of the car. I make a coffee from the thermos I keep in the boot for just these occasions, and wait for what I hope will be others for the tour. The trees tower around me like great sentinels. Huge tree ferns fill the space between the trunks and birds flit in and out.

Another car arrives, a couple with a boy around nine and a girl, a bit younger. I'm glad. Children add an extra dimension, often asking questions adults wouldn't think of or would be embarrassed to ask. We trudge down a muddy track to a wooden shelter in the bush, to join a man and two middle-aged women from London. Now, *that* puts my question of whether to spend time driving the extra 12 kilometres into perspective.

'Everyone rugged up?' says the guide. He opens a gate and we enter the coldly still darkness of the cave. Bending beneath an overhanging ledge, we follow the torch light along a narrow walkway. We stand upright.

'Ooh, Mummy,' breathes the little girl, 'it's like a fairy palace.' Stalactites of every form descend from the roof: spears, metres long, thick white tubes and delicate straws like icicles. Stalagmites rise from the floor, cone-shaped, reaching up to their creators, some already joined and thick around the middle. The guide turns to us.

'Cave formations are created when calcium carbonate in the rain water seeps through cracks in the earth's surface. It hits the damp air of the cave and forms calcite crystals. Each drip of water deposits more calcite, creating a tiny tube, like a drinking straw. As the centre of the straw fills up, the water runs down its sides and it become thicker and longer. That's how you get stalactites.'

'What about the ones sticking up from the floor,' asks the boy.

'Good question,' says the guide. 'The stalactites drip onto the floor and the calcite builds up there and becomes stalagmites. After a very long time, the two meet. You'll see plenty of the columns and pillars where they've met as we go around.' The boy's father puts him arm around his son's shoulder, proud of him for asking the question. The further we go, the more elaborate the decorations become. Huge calcite shawls unfurl elegantly from the ceiling, fold upon fold, like giant curtains, some pure white, some streaked with pale browns.

He leads us around a thick column, fenced off from destructive hands. 'When people first started coming here, they used to run their hands along the formations – even break bits off.' He shudders. It is a horrible thought, though I can understand someone wanting a piece of this beautiful calcite. 'The oil from human hands causes the water to bypass the spot that is touched and without water the formation is damaged.' We amble past a massive rock, sparkling with calcite, as if covered in diamonds. My 'New Age', crystal-loving friends, would go mad in here.

I squeeze my way through tight fissures between limestone walls and around blind corners, ruminating on the stress I experience driving my car around a mountainous road, or standing on a platform only moderately high off the ground. Yet I can be trapped with minimal lighting inside the earth and be completely comfortable. A fear of heights should denote a nervous person who would be frightened of everything, but not so, luckily. If you were frightened of heights *and* claustrophobic, life would be a lot more difficult.

The green of the forest greets us. There's a longer way back to the car park, a track through the bush. In two days I will be back in my house in the city and so I take the opportunity of boosting my rain forest intake in preparation for that. It's warmer amongst the trees.

Tiny birds dart in and out. I try to catch a good look at them but they're too quick and zip away before I get the chance. I trip over a tree root and as I right myself, a strange thumping echoes from somewhere. I intuitively reach out for something to hold onto, which turns out to be the delicate frond of a fern. The earth vibrates, there's a great smashing and crashing in the undergrowth. A huge kangaroo passes within feet of me. It's gone as quickly as it came. I brace myself against a tree and allow my heart to return to normal.

I realise now, that I probably shouldn't have taken this path. I only have 20 minutes to get back to *Marakoopa* for the next tour. I start to run, scrambling over fallen branches and tree roots, back uphill and out into the empty car park. I'm suddenly very keen to see the river cave and the glow worms. I'll be very annoyed with myself if I'm too late. Perhaps they'll hold the tour up for me; *that* will be embarrassing. I get upset with people that turn up late for things, considering that if I can get there on time, why can't they? I arrive, red-faced and panting, with two minutes to spare. The family is here again, along with a couple from France and two young Australian men.

The caves *are* quite different. This one is not as decorative, for the simple reason that *King Solomons* is close to the surface and so more water leaches through. It's still gorgeous, though. 'Oohs' and 'aahs' issue from around me. It's odd to be inside the earth and have a river running beneath you. I've never given a thought to underground rivers before. It rustles in the dark below us. The children become braver as we go along and halfway through they are comfortable enough to move around, rather than clinging to their parents. The girl leans over the railing to look into the river and her mother moves closer. 'Be careful.' The child ignores her, knowing she's safe.

'When will we see the glow worms,' asks the boy.

'Not yet, mate.'

Marakoopa and *King Solomons* are just two caves in an area that contains over 300 caves and sinkholes. Both are home to a range of fascinating animals – fish, shrimp, crayfish, salamanders, snails and insects – which have evolved features that allow them to adapt to their lightless environments.

'A lot of our creatures in here have no skin colour and no eyes,' says the guide. The little girl pops her eyes at her mother.

'How do they see?' she whispers.

'They don't need to see,' he says. 'It's completely dark in caves so they rely on their sense of touch to get around. I'll give you an idea of what it's like to be them.' He dims the lights, they turn off completely, and darkness smothers us. A thrill of fear ripples through the group. No-one moves and I immediately worry for the children, even though they have their own parents to worry about them. The lighting returns with audible sighs of relief. The guide is very nice but I'm sure he waits with delight for that bit.

An enormous chamber, a natural cathedral, opens out around us. Shawls unfold and drape themselves across massive rocks, criss-crossing other formations to create new and more spectacular shapes. Ancient pillars appear to be supporting the roof, which is covered by a lacework of millions of miniature fibres, tiny stalactites just beginning their journey.

'That's flowstone,' he says, pointing to what looks like a crop of gigantic mushrooms, growing out of the wall. 'Flowstone is caused by running water, rather than the drips of stalactites. The minerals build up in thin layers which take on the shape of the floor and the walls around them.' A massive flowstone spills across the floor like a beautiful white river.

'Is it time for the glow worms, yet,' asks the boy.

'Not yet, mate. We have to see the wedding cake first.' We descend some steps and stand before a large formation squeezed between the overhanging roof and a limestone ledge beside us. It's almost as wide as it is tall. Water has trickled down its sides, creating patterns that look exactly like rivulets of soft white icing. I wonder for a moment how long it took this to form but quickly give it away. Cave stalactites are the fastest growing, but that's still only around an inch a year.

'Okay guys, follow me and we'll see if we can find some glow worms.' The children push to the front. 'Now, if you look up there, I'll turn the lights down. Are you ready?' We all nod, like a group of school children. The light dims and disappears and the roof twinkles with millions of stars. The group emits a collective sigh. Glow worms are theatrical in this situation but they're not the most attractive of creatures. They are actually the larvae of mosquito-like flies. They hang from the ceiling in little tubes, dropping strings dotted with droplets of sticky mucus, not unlike spiders' webs.

'Glow worms have a light they can turn on to attract insects. Where do you think the light comes from, kids?' No hands go up. 'Their bottoms.'

'Eeewww,' say the children, together. The two young men snigger.

'Insects come to check out the lights – maybe they think there's a party – they get stuck on the strings and that's the end of them. They get gobbled up by the glow worms.' It's the grand finale. The stars fade and disappear as the lights come up. The gate is opened and we return to our own world.

***

It's late afternoon at Latrobe and the sign on the pub says *Vacancy $35*. It's a bit rough-looking but for $35 I can handle it.

'I'm looking for a room for the night,' I say to the man behind the bar. He looks at me as if I was born specifically to upset his day. He finishes serving beer to two men who look like that's the last thing they need and comes back.

'$35,' he says. I hand him the cash. 'Wait here.' He disappears into a corridor and returns frowning and tense, to the bar, without looking at me. I don't think he's too happy in his work. A young, nervous-looking woman follows in his wake.

'I'll take you up,' she says. The room is just that, a room with a bed, which is fine, except that I don't think their customers have been following the 'no smoking' rule – or they haven't bothered installing one. I walk into a solid fog of stale cigarettes. I didn't expect luxury but I did expect to be able to breathe. It's not much to ask, after all, even for $35. The window is open very slightly so at least I won't die of lack of oxygen. There should be enough to sustain me for a few hours.

It's already dark as I venture out onto the street to look for something to eat. I'm usually anxious about bringing hot food into a hotel room because of the smell it might leave but this, of course, does not apply tonight. It will just add to what's already there, maybe make an interesting mix. Chicken, a roast potato, cooked who knows how long ago, and some watery peas make up my dinner. Watery gravy covers the lot. All is forgiven when I discover an electric blanket. I can handle anything as long as I'm warm. I relax into sleep, disturbed only by the odd whiff of *Gravox* and a very strange dream about a chimney sweep.

***

If you want to know what heaven is, indulge yourself with hot chocolate made in a chocolate factory: pure liquid chocolate. *Anvers Chocolate Factory* is situated in a beautiful Californian bungalow, surrounded by cottage gardens. I have trouble getting the attention of the two women behind the counter. They seem to have a problem – something has upset them and they're not concentrating. It's assertiveness time or I could be here all day.

'Should I go in?' I ask, waving my hand at the dining room. One of them nods, but the grumpy look remains on her face. I sit next to a window and survey the menu. A waitress walks past and I'm too slow on the uptake to halt her progress. On her second time around, I call out and order my liquid heaven. The room is cold but the light morning sun shines through, emulating warmth. Tonight I catch the boat home but I still have the day to fill in and I'm pretty sure a couple of hours will take care of Devonport. Maybe I could flit up to Burnie for the morning.

The 'Factory' is also a museum, showing the history of chocolate and many of the implements used for its manufacture through the years. Cocoa originated in the Amazon, at least 4000 years ago. In both the Mayan and Aztec cultures, it was the basis of a cold, unsweetened drink, believed to be a health elixir. Sugar was unknown and so they used different spices to add flavour, even hot chilli peppers. To the Mayans, cacao pods symbolised life and fertility. They believed that wisdom and power came from eating the fruit of the cocao tree, and that it had nourishing, fortifying and even aphrodisiac qualities.

The beans were also used as currency. In 1513, 100 cocoa beans bought a slave, 10 bought the services of a prostitute and four got you a rabbit for your dinner. In 1528, the Spaniard, Hernando Cortez, who disliked its bitterness, added sugar and its use spread throughout Europe. In the mid 1600s, France's Louis *XIV*, organised its manufacture as a new income stream, but also for its capacity to inspire erotic pleasures. It's well known that Louis, in his 72nd year, was making love to his wife twice a day. Now there's a thought! Casanova used chocolate with champagne to seduce his ladies and the well-known nymphomaniac, Madame du Barry, encouraged her lovers to drink chocolate in order to keep up with her.

Solid chocolate was developed in England in 1830 and smooth and velvety replaced course-grained in 1847. The Swiss added milk in 1875, creating what we indulge in today. So, there you have it. If you want to be healthy and have a good love life, eat chocolate.

Chapter 6

It's a relief to be on my first freeway for nearly two weeks. As much as I love forested mountains, driving around them can be exhausting. The paddocks and hills fly by. Burnie is not somewhere I would have considered a tourist destination but it has a very interesting history. It began its life as Emu Bay, named after the sub-species of emu, smaller than its mainland counterparts, that roamed the district at the time of settlement. The first permanent settlers arrived on the vessel, *Caroline*, in February, 1828, and began carving out a village from the dense rainforest and tea-tree swamps. They established a saw mill and Burnie became a timber port, exporting timber to Melbourne, Adelaide and Launceston, for every- thing from roof shingles to road paving, house building to ship building.

In the 1870s, a wooden, horse-drawn tramway was built to haul tin from the Mt. Bischoff Tin Mine, 75 kilometres away at Waratah. The tramway was converted to steam locomotives in the late 1880s and extended to Zeehan to service the mineral boom in the north-west. The port expanded and Burnie flourished.

By 1915, the mines had declined and the town fell back on forestry and farming for its existence. Some form of secondary industry was needed and in the late 1930s, the entrepreneur, Gerald Mussen, established *Australian Pulp and Paper Mills Ltd*. The company looked after its employees well. Mussen wrote: "The human element in commerce and industry must have first consideration, and profit must be placed second. If the employees feel that they are not fairly treated, no monetary reward will induce them to give their fullest production." By 1965, the population had grown to 18,500.

In the 1970s, the Whitlam Government reduced import duties and re-valued the dollar by 7%, making it much more difficult for the mill to compete with overseas product. The company began downsizing and in 1993, after bitter industrial disputes over wage claims, it was sold off. It's a very sad ending for a company that began its life with the well-being of the employees paramount.

Burnie bounced back again. It now has a strong base, manufacturing equipment for the north-west's underground mining, and exporting its products to 65 countries around the world. Only an hour from the mainland, it's become the fifth largest container port in Australia. It has a totally different look and feel to anywhere else I've been on this trip. Docks are normally set a distance away from the general goings-on of the city but not here. It's an odd experience standing at one end of the main street with a huge ship filling the landscape at the other. A sign outside the *Returned and Services League Club* advertises lunch. The dining room is empty, except for a man, probably in his late 70s, sitting alone at a table.

'Anywhere you like, love,' says a woman, as I enter. The room has the well-used look of an *RSL*: the floral carpet has been cleaned of many a spill, the tables are laminated and the chairs, vinyl. I choose a spot two tables away from the man. He watches me as I remove my coat and look around. The woman has disappeared.

'Do we order at the bar,' I ask.

'Yes.' He explains the menu to me and tells me today is 'seniors specials' day.

'Great. I've just become a 'senior'. I'll take advantage of it.' I move to the bar and he joins me. The woman reappears and takes our orders and we return to our tables. He continues looking across at me and I take the hint.

'You live around here?'

'Forty years,' he says. We throw comments to and fro. I realise I'll have to do something about the situation – we can't yell at each other all through lunch. It's a risk, asking someone to join you. You may end up having nothing to say to each other after all but I take the plunge.

'You come over here,' he says, without moving. Of course, he's of the era when men do the inviting. I grab my coat and bag and move across. 'I lost my wife five years ago,' he says.

'Oh ... sad.' I should have come up with something better but I was caught by surprise. 'Was she ill?' Of course she was ill. She wouldn't have been old enough to die naturally. He nods.

'It was just the two of us.'

'Right ... you didn't have children?' He looks at me sharply, as if I'm being critical. 'People don't have to have children, do they?' An attempt to smooth the waters. He looks away. This is not going well.

'I've got a dog,' he says.

'What sort?'

'Shih Tzu x King Charles Spaniel.'

'Lovely.'

'We go for walks each morning.' The woman arrives with our food.

'I see you've moved,' she says to me, giving him a knowing look, as if it's a regular manipulation of his to get people to join him. And why not? Why shouldn't he have company for lunch if he wants to?

'You won't charge me too much, will you?' he says to her.

'You say that every time, Reg.' I'm insulted for him. Okay, he might say the same thing every time, but that doesn't give her the right to treat him rudely. I consider advising her of the fact but she charges away and it's no longer my business. Probably not my business in the first place, considering he didn't care at all. I tuck into my fish, chips and what these days is called salad – lettuce leaves hiding two cherry tomato halves and a slice of cucumber.

'So, you haven't considered remarrying?' I only asked it to fill a gap in the conversation, being the sort of person that gaps in conversations make very nervous. His mouth drops open, revealing two lumps of pork, as yet not fully chewed. I've crossed a line that this generation takes for granted. 'Sorry. A bit personal?'

'Yes, it is.' He allows me suffer in silence for a couple of minutes.

'Are you married?' he asks.

'No, divorced.' He's shocked and a little disdainful, as if I've let the team down. Our relationship has hit rock bottom. He pushes his plate away and I take the opportunity to escape.

'I'd better get going. I'm catching the boat back tonight.' He turns away and I'm forgotten.

***

Devonport's long main street is like any other, a mall in the centre, lined with chain stores: *Target, Suzanne Grae, Just Jeans.* I wander around the hilly streets for a while till the vicious wind sends me back to the car. At the beach on the other side of the river, I make a last thermos coffee and look out across Bass Strait. At six in the morning, the skyscrapers of my city will greet me and I will crawl through peak-hour traffic to my cottage in the south-east. Do I want to go home? Not really. One of the challenges of travelling is that, while everyday life is put on hold for a time, it has to be returned to, and everyday life is often not nearly as interesting as travelling. I guess the trick is to have a life that you want to go back to, one that is already interesting and challenging, in which case, travelling would be an addition to, rather than an escape from.

It's already dark as I sit in the queue, my little red hatchback surrounded by camper vans, SUV's and motor bikes. My daughter booked me onto an overnight recliner, but in her capacity as travel agent, informed the company it was a birthday gift and an upgrade would be looked on kindly. *There's an off chance*, she'd said to me. *After all, it's winter; they won't be booked out.*

It worked going over. I've got my fingers crossed it will work again.

'There you are, Coral,' says the woman at the booth, 'you've been upgraded to a cabin.'

'By myself?' I ask. I'm not sure of the situation. I may end up with some bloke with bad wind and a snore reminiscent of a fog horn.

'Of course,' she says, smiling as if she's read my mind. 'Enjoy your night.' The van behind urges me forward toward the ramp that will take me high above the river onto the ship. The town spreads out around me. I desperately want to shut my eyes until it's over but that's probably not the best decision in the circumstances. I crawl and bump my way over the joins in the ramp to the other side and follow directions to where my car will spend the night.

The lights of Devonport twinkle. I finish off a second wine, leave my glass on the bar and enter the rabbit warren of passages that contain the cabins, their doors all exactly the same. I find mine after only two tries, not bad, considering I'm a very cheap drunk. I curl up in my bunk, thoughts rumbling. I left a job a month before coming and so, at this moment, I have no income and no idea of what the future holds. Friends have often said I should write my ideas down, my ideas being considered unusual, a little left-of-centre, they say, whatever that means. They've never seemed unusual to me. In fact, they made perfect sense and so, other than odd scrapings in a journal to keep my mind in order, I've managed to avoid it.

I come from a family of story-tellers – two of my siblings are poets and my father writes novels. Maybe it's time to join in. From an early age I've wanted to explore, to see the world as it's lived outside of my own tiny sphere and now, being past middle-age and responsible for no-one, I have the chance. Maybe I could add writing to it, tell stories of what I see and experience. In Tassie that would be the divine forests and caves, the mountains and rivers, the coastline constantly changing and the fascinating history, black and white, not so far in the past. Would anyone want to read them? Don't know. Does it matter? Not sure. The ship sinks deeper into the waves and, as if I'm in a cradle, rocks me to sleep.

July 2009

Chapter 7

The *Spirit of Tasmania* docks at Devonport at 6.30am and by 7.30am I'm on my way. I'm returning to Tassie for another look. This time I've planned to the nth degree to avoid the mistakes of my last trip, in particular, finding myself at the end of the day on a mountain in the dark, the petrol tank on empty and nowhere to stay. The car has been completely checked and I'm assured there will be no problems with it. I have a horror of breaking down on a deserted mountainside, especially with no certainty of mobile connection to ring for help.

I feel good, not too tired, surprising, considering I've had a long night. My first experience of the luxury recliners on the ship was not a good one. It can't be an accident that seats are that uncomfortable; someone has to have put a lot of time and thought into it. I battled with the lever for ages before realising that the footrest only goes up halfway, preventing the comfortable resting of the feet and putting terrific pressure on the lower back. Along with that, the reading lamp is set into one armrest in such a position that it precludes the resting of the arm. So, if you can sleep with your feet dangling six inches off the floor and your arms crossed over your chest, you're fine. I can't.

I've never wandered around a ship in the middle of the night. It's a strange experience, a touch dreamlike, as if you're in a capsule, which I suppose you are, separated from the world, a more comfortable version of what it must have been like on the sailing ships, cut off from all communication. Our televisions still buzzed away, though, overseeing others who decided to see out the trip sitting up. There's a rule against sleeping on the couches but it's obviously very flexible. Several young men were too 'under the weather' to make it any further. Couples chatted quietly, a barman hummed along to the music as he polished his last glass. At 2am, I tried to sleep again – I'd planned to explore Rocky Cape National Park on my way through to my first night in Stanley on the north-west coast – but the snores from the bodies draped around me were reaching a crescendo, and I was reminded of one of the reasons I'm single.

***

My father was keen to check out the little town of Penguin when he and my mother were here. He's a bit of an explorer, like myself, but my mother's idea of exploration is finding the best coffee shop. I can imagine the debate between them as they approached the turnoff from the highway. My father lost and was quietly disappointed so I promised to pop in and send him a postcard. The *Penguin Uniting Church* sits at the beginning of the main drag, looking out across Bass Strait. Its cream, wooden walls are enclosed by a deep rust-red roof, set in a series of steep gables. A square tower and spire are slotted into one side, topped with the same red roof. It gleams in the morning sun.

A sign directs me to a Sunday market. Lucky timing – I love country markets. This one is disappointing, though, mostly second-hand goods masquerading as antiques. There's a very nice crystal stall though, and I complain to the woman about the seats on the ship. She understands – Tasmanians use The *Spirit* as a bus service. I buy some tumblers and a little rose quartz pyramid, stop at a jewellery store and, again, take the opportunity to whinge.

'I take a bag,' says the woman, 'put old stuff in it and support my legs on that.'

'Thanks,' I say, 'I'll try it.'

***

It's a funny thing that any time I decide to shout myself a pleasant eating experience, I can't find one. I've ended up in the bakery with a packet sandwich, expensive and tasteless, and *Nescafe* instant coffee. I force down the sandwich to allay my hunger pangs and leave the coffee behind. As I do a circuit of the town before leaving, I see a beautiful cafe right near the market. How did I miss it? I must be tireder than I thought. It's 10.30am and I've been on the road for three hours. I suddenly feel sick – really sick. The further I drive the worse I feel. The docklands of Burnie disappear in a haze. I'll have to miss Rocky Cape; maybe I can do it on the way back. I can see The Nut, my signal that Stanley is not too far away. My vision is slightly blurred and I feel weirdly out of balance.

I probably shouldn't still be driving but there's no-one around and I'm on the home stretch.

'They're still cleaning the rooms,' says the girl at the reception desk of the Stanley Hotel where I'm booked for two nights.

'I didn't get any sleep on the boat,' I say, 'and I feel really sick.' She can tell I'm not acting.

'I'll check. Maybe there's one ready.' There's nowhere to sit down so I lean on the counter.

'You can go up,' she says, handing me a key. I collapse on the bed and sleep for three hours.

***

My little yellow room is freshly painted and double doors lead out onto the balcony that surrounds the hotel. Leaning over the beautiful, wrought-iron balustrade, it's easy to imagine I'm back in the 1800s. Take away my car and a couple of others and replace them with wagons and maybe a *Cobb & Co* coach and I'm there. I set out for a look around. Stanley sits at the base of an unusual land formation known as The Nut, the stump of an ancient volcano. It was first sighted by explorers, Matthew Flinders and George Bass. Flinders wrote that he had seen a "cliffy, round lump, resembling a Christmas Cake," and named it Circular Head.

In 1824, a group of London merchants created the *Van Diemen's Land Company*, with a view to growing wool to supply the British textile industry. They were granted 250,000 acres of land in the north-west, with Circular Head as its centre of operations. Stud livestock, implements, craftsmen and indentured labourers from

England, along with local convicts, landed in 1826. The port opened in 1827 but development was slow, as approval for anything had to come from London where the company was based. In the meantime, cold destroyed the stock, crops perished in the damp climate and servants absconded. In the 1840s, the company gave in, and began selling and leasing its holdings. It is now confined mainly to its *Woolnorth* property, west of Smithton.

Stanley was designed by John Lee Archer in the 1840s, and named after Lord Stanley, British Secretary of State for the Colonies. Its main industries are fishing and tourism. The wide main street is rimmed by stone cottages, many of them now 'Bed and Breakfasts'. One is *Lyons Cottage*, the birthplace of Joseph Lyons, Prime Minister of Australia between 1932 and his death in 1939. He was known as 'Honest Joe', for providing stable leadership through the Great Depression. I wander past the war memorial and the railway station that serviced the port, now also accommodation. It's the most spotless town I've ever been in but I always find this degree of cleanliness a little sinister. I wonder what would happen if I forgot myself and dropped a lolly paper. I have a vision of a team from Special Forces descending from helicopters and whisking me off to a gulag.

Back at the hotel, the bistro is filling up. A log fire burns in the corner and Michael Bublé sings quietly in the background. A sign, 'Best Bistro in Australia 2008', sits on the bar.

'Gave us a huge shock,' says the waitress. 'We really didn't expect it.' I'm treated as the most important person in the world, the food is delicious and the Tasmanian

Pinot, to die for. I've been in more beautiful places than this – the chairs are black vinyl and laminated wood surrounds the bar – but it's definitely the most delightful dining experience I've ever had. One of the disadvantages of travelling alone is feeling you need to leave a place once you've finished your meal, rather than remaining, looking, I always suspect, like a bit of a loser. I climb the back stairs to my room.

***

The Stranded Whale, opposite the hotel, serves breakfast. Everything here has an ocean theme, naturally, as the town, being on an isthmus, is surrounded by water. I'm heading up to the historic estate of *Highfield*. I'll need some sustenance, as I spend ages at these places, thanks to my enlightened grade 6 teacher, Mr. Moir, who turned Australian history into an adventure. I still remember our class in the tiny Gippsland town of Longwarry, mapping the treks of the early explorers: Eyre, Sturt, Burke and Wills.

My project was Ludwig Leichhardt, who left Sydney for Brisbane in August 1844, to search for a harbour at the head of the Gulf of Carpentaria, mapping and naming as he went. The Government had the view of establishing a trading route between the settled parts of New South Wales and the islands of the eastern Archipelago and Asia. He reached Port Essington on the north-west tip of Arnhem Land on December 17th 1845, but disappeared later on an expedition to cross the continent from Brisbane to Perth. His fate remains a mystery. I'm still a little in love with Ludwig.

I order scrambled eggs. The woman is middle-aged, and strong and independent-looking. 'I've been working on the mainland for years,' she says, 'but I wanted to get back. The cafe came on the market and so I bought it.'

'It's a beautiful little town. Very quiet.'

'It's off season.' I take another opportunity to question the seats on The *Spirit*. She commiserates and suggests booking a share cabin and hoping no-one else turns up. 'It's worked for me,' she says, 'and after all, you're actually closer to people in the seats than in a cabin.'

'True, but it's something about beds. Seems more intimate?' She leaves that hanging and turns away to read the paper.

***

'We receive much less money from the Government than some of the more well-known estates,' says the enthusiastic young woman, as I stare through the sitting room window across mile after mile of lush, undulating pastures, finishing abruptly at the ocean in the distance, 'and so the refurbishment of the house is a slow work in progress.'

Highfield House was built for Edward Curr, chief agent of the *Van Diemen's Land Company*, between 1832 and 1835. Prior to this, he had lived in a weatherboard cottage. Curr wrote in July, 1832: "The wooden house I live in will not stand 15 years; the stone one which I am building will stand a century." It was constructed in the Regency style (1811-1820), characterised by decoration that's geometric but elegant. Historians considered this period as the coming together of the 'Age of Reason', with its focus on knowledge and rationality, and Romanticism, which created a yearning for travel, nature and poetry. Large French windows allow light into the main rooms and take in sweeping views of Bass Strait. And so, 'the light of reason' shines through while, simultaneously, the attention is drawn to the dramatic view.

This is all very well, but I'm sure all Mrs. Curr was interested in was somewhere to install her rapidly-expanding family. Elizabeth had 15 children in 23 years. In 1838, the roof space was converted into attic sleeping rooms for her daughters. In 1844, John Lee Archer was hired to design further extensions, including servants' rooms and a new kitchen. It's not unlike what most of us have done at some stage, extended our house to accommodate a growing family, though many of the children of the early colonists were dispatched to boarding schools in England. Some were as young as three – education was obviously more important than love. I wonder how the women felt having to send their children away like packages. And what effect did it have on the children? It's too horrible to think about.

It's not a large house as some historic mansions go, but it *is* very elegant, with timber shutters and marble fireplaces, and verandas surrounded by decorative iron lacework. I don't mind that restoration is still underway. I'm sure it would never have been in a perfect state, anyway, housing a busy family of that size. In 1853, its future as home to the chief agent was reassessed. The company relocated to Burnie and the house was privately leased. The Tasmanian Government bought in 1982.

I stroll into the garden along a pathway to an alcove containing a tomb. In 1838, Curr's two-year-old daughter, Juliana, had been riding in a cart harnessed to a dog. The dog rushed to fight with other dogs outside the yard, causing her to hit her head on the fencing. The monument is surrounded by honeysuckle and sweet briar.

On the way back, I stop at a lookout. As the territory of the *Parpeloihener* and *Pennemukeer* peoples, it was first invaded by sealers, who competed for resources such as mutton birds, seals and shellfish, and who forcibly abducted the tribes' women. By 1828, battle was raging all over the colony between the aborigines and the settlers. In an attempt to ease the hostilities, Governor Arthur enacted a law. Aborigines were forbidden to enter settled districts of the colony unless they had a pass signed and sealed by him. Needless to say, the natives weren't happy with the deal. At the culmination of a series of violent clashes, four shepherds from the Van Dieman's Land Company massacred 30 aborigines at Cape Grimm, and hurled their bodies over the 60 metre cliff. The shepherds then named the spot, Victory Hill.

As the responsible magistrate, Edward Curr disputed the numbers killed, did not initiate an investigation and didn't even report the incident to Governor Arthur. He wrote to the directors of the *Van Dieman's Land Company*: "... but I saw first that there was a strong presumption that our men were right, second if wrong it was impossible to convict them, and thirdly that the mere enquiry would induce every man to leave Cape Grimm." It's now farming country, very beautiful, soft and quiet. All I can hear are the waves breaking on the shoreline and some chooks in the farm next to me.

***

Stanley's old cemetery stands on a hill looking out towards the ocean. The spot must have been chosen deliberately. People of those times seemed to have had a feel for the theatrical, as its position adds to its poignancy. Gravestones describe the deaths of whole families from the 1800s on, children only weeks old, wives lost in childbirth and replaced by others, lost in the same way. Few made it to old age.

I order the same meal and wine at the bistro and sit at the same table. 'It's like déjà vu,' says the waitress from the night before.

Chapter 8

It's the edge of the world. That's what the sign says and, standing on this hill looking out to sea, that's how it feels. Untamed and untameable: Arthur River, North-West Tasmania. If you sailed from where the river enters the sea and kept going, you would hit South America without touching land. This accounts for the vicious wind ripping through me and I'm grateful for the knitted beanie a caring friend gave me on my announcement that I was exploring Tassie in the depths of winter. I was looking to book in for the river cruise but I had an inkling, when I saw the boat in the back yard of the company's premises, that the cruise might be was off.

'I wish companies would put their 'down' times in their brochures,' I whined to the woman behind the counter in the dingy office.

'No, it's not in our brochures,' she said, put out a little by my criticism, 'but it's *definitely* on our web site.' *I* hadn't seen it. I'll check when I get home.

Tasmanians have a habit of not mentioning that, for a few weeks in July, they close everything up and disappear, underground maybe, or into caves; or, as someone suggested, to catch up on shopping in Melbourne.

The woman at the cabin park certainly didn't say, before booking me in and disappearing to New Zealand. 'I'm just the caretaker,' said the man when I arrived, 'I don't know anything,' at which point he vanished into a house behind a large hedge and I hadn't seen him since.

I'm disappointed about the river cruise but I've done road trips often enough to know that adversity can be changed to opportunity. My main reason for coming here is to experience the ancient north-west forests, recently named the Tarkine Wilderness. I'll now have an extra day for that. I stop by the take-away shop, the only one in Arthur River, on the way back to setting myself up comfortably in my cabin. *Closed,* says the sign. Luckily, I'd been told to bring food, so I cook up my 2 minute noodles and set myself up next to the heater to relax and read. It's a beautiful little cabin, almost new and just perfect for one person. A red feature wall faces me to help keep my spirits up on this grey day and I know I'm going to be comfortable for the three nights I'm here.

It starts drizzling around four but I'm not worried about it. It'll take more than a shower to stop me. My next two days *are* going to be spent in the forest. Drizzle turns to rain and rain to deluge. I wonder how stable the cabin is. I have a picture of it floating, me inside clinging precariously to the bed, down the hill to the mouth of the river and out to sea; next stop, Cape Horn. I wonder how long it takes to get there. My plans for spending tomorrow in the forest are fading fast. The television is not coping with the weather, and so I make myself some toast, have a quick shower and adjourn to bed to wait it out.

The storm that wakes me could also wake the dead. The sky lights up again and again, lightning bolts advancing nearer and nearer to where I'm lying. Thunder rolls, thumps and pounds. Mother Earth is flaunting her power. It's an eerie experience being alone in a cabin park during a storm. It's deafeningly noisy and quiet at the same time. I need the toilet but that's not going to happen. No way am *I* going to be hit by lightning while on the toilet. A girl has her pride. I hate storms at home but, strangely, I'm not a bit afraid. It's like being in a cocoon, protected and safe, while the world rages around me. I start wondering if I *should* be afraid. Maybe I *am* in danger and don't realise it. What if I was hit by lightning and no-one knew? There *is* a tree between me and the next cabin. Don't trees attract lightning? An explosion together with an almighty flash, as if from some huge camera, is followed by the shuddering of the earth, then another, so close I think it's hit the window, though I suppose if it had I wouldn't still be sitting here.

That's it, the grand finale. The onslaught eases away to a steady downpour and Mother Nature goes to sleep. The lamp above the bed is dead. I crawl off the mattress and try the light switch. The electricity is gone. I find when I open the curtains that it's 7.30 and daylight. Without electricity I have no heating, cooking, radio or television. I pour myself a bowl of cereal while waiting for the rain to ease, then don my runners, pluck my umbrella from the car, congratulating myself on having thought to bring it, and plough out into the river that is the park roadway and across to the kiosk to ring the caretaker. There's no answer. An hour later I try again. Nothing.

That's when I notice the van, parked next to the kiosk yesterday, is gone.

I would be quite happy to stay in this beautiful spot by myself but without electricity the room is cold and getting colder, the rain is still heavy and showing no sign of abating and I realise I'll have to give in and leave. I pack my gear back in the car, leave a note with $70 for the night, and head back in the direction I came from. I'm halfway to Burnie before I realise that all I probably had to do was turn the fuse back on in the meter box, located, conveniently, next to the fridge.

***

I'm sitting at a table in a dark petrol station convenience store with a lukewarm coffee. A text has come from my sister asking how my trip is going and I'm trying to explain my Arthur River experience. Texting is fabulous for keeping up with people but limited when it comes to writing essays. The rain has eased and I actually think that's sunshine peeping through the curtains. I'm heading for Rocky Cape National Park though I'm not in the mood. I'm devastated that I'm on a highway when I could have been in a forest.

I bought a *National Parks* pass on The *Spirit* but there's no entrance gate and no-one to show it to. The landscape has changed completely from trees and green paddocks to rather bleak coastal shrubbery. The dirt road seems to go for miles before reaching the red-stained, grey rocky cliffs of the coastline. I follow a walking track up a hill and come to an historic sight, a cave used by indigenous tribes for thousands of years. It starts drizzling and I'd love to sneak in and sit there as they did, maybe feel some sort of connection, but it's fenced off.

The car has a rattle – I can hear it somewhere around the back wheels. Am I imagining it? I'm always imagining car noises. It's because I know nothing about cars and so I need to worry in *case* something's wrong. The worst thing that can happen to me is to break down, especially in the middle of nowhere. This is definitely the middle of nowhere. I haven't seen another vehicle since I came into the Park. I'll feel safer on the main road where there's a chance of a mobile signal to ring the *Royal Automobile Club of Tasmania* for help. Please God, let me get back to the road and I'll be good forever. I make a decision; no more parks or, at least, gravel roads. The risk is too great. This is another huge disappointment. National Parks are the main reason I came. The rain increases and, with it, my mood drops further.

***

I've rung the cabin park at Port Sorell and brought my stay forward two days. 'You're at the wrong place,' says the woman. 'That park is a few blocks further into town.' The rain is now so heavy I can hardly see through the windscreen. The very last thing I want to do is keep driving. 'Actually,' she says, her voice low, 'it's got a bit of a reputation.'

'Has it?'

'Well, you hear things.' I wonder what she's heard. 'You can ask to see the room and if you don't like it, come back here.' *That* would take assertiveness and in my present frame of mind, I couldn't rustle up the energy.

My brain battles at any time with greyness and cold, without adding tiredness to it. 'I could ring them for you,' she offers, 'make your excuses.'

These are the decisions you make when you're on the road and all your plans have gone up the spout and it's pouring and you're freezing. The cabin is old, with walls of dark wood laminate, popular in the 70s but never good for lifting the spirits, chips in the bathroom sink and *bad* draughts. It *is* the coldest place I've ever spent a night, and that includes Gippsland. The park is located alongside the local footy ground, very convenient if you want to watch the football from your bedroom window but not good for protection from the wind. A floor heater, wall radiator, clothes and a doona and blanket just keep me alive.

I get up early to escape, noticing the water around the inside of the bedroom window, wash the ice off the car and leave, too angry to acknowledge the woman who talked me into it. The rain has stopped, making it easy to find the Port Sorell Cabin Park where I was originally booked. It's beautiful, spotless and almost new. I follow the signs to the beach, marvelling that no matter where I go, the view is straight off a postcard. I walk for a while in the morning sunshine and relax from the disappointments of the day before. My anger eases and I realise the woman at the cabin park definitely thought she was helping me out. I just think it's time she had a fresh look at some of her cabins.

Chapter 9

I cut across to Exeter then up the Tamar Valley to Beaconsfield. On 25th April 2006, 17 miners were involved in a rock fall while working underground at the gold mine. Fourteen escaped. At the time, Larry Knight was almost a kilometre underground driving a teleoader, a vehicle with a protective basket on the end of an arm. Brant Webb and Todd Russell were in the basket, applying steel mesh to the tunnel wall to prevent rock falls. Knight was killed but Webb and Russell were protected by the basket, though they were partially buried under rocks. The two men were trapped for the next fortnight while complicated planning and dangerous blasting and drilling were instigated to try and save them. They were rescued on Tuesday 9th May.

In the meantime, media had come from everywhere, swarming over the town and making it the focus of world attention. I want to know what effect this experience would have on a community, if there's a residue, some sort of atmosphere, maybe, that can be picked up on. A new visitor centre has been built. Entry to the museum is expensive and I'm not interested enough in mining equipment to pay the price. I study the memorial, unveiled by Prime Minister John Howard in July, 2006. It seems cold and separated, somehow, from the enormity of what happened, though I don't know what more could be done.

A meeting of the *Australian Workers' Union*, held on the 15th May, 2006, reported that miners had been unhappy with the reductions in the amount of cement used to close in exploited parts of the mine. Supports were removed from lower parts and mesh intended to prevent rock collapse was known to be ineffective. The Government investigation in 2006 determined the rock fall occurred as a result of 'unexpected seismic activity induced by mining activities'. In 2009, the Tasmanian coroner concluded that it could not have been predicted, nor could Beaconsfield Mine be held responsible for the death of Larry Knight. I guess we'll never know.

I choose a tiny deli for my morning coffee. Two small, round tables are already occupied and the only alternative I have is to join a woman at one of them. She's reading a book so I leave her to it.

'You from around here?' she says, after a few minutes.

'No, I've just arrived. I'm from Melbourne.' I realised some time ago that I was missing out on the full travel experience by not interacting with people along the way and so I'm opening myself up when the chance arises. This is definitely one of those times. 'Are you a local?' I ask.

'Yes, I run a dairy farm a few miles out but I grew up in Victoria.'

'Where was that?'

'Korumburra in South Gippsland.'

'*Really*? I grew up in Drouin ... West Gippsland. Went to school in Warragul.'

'It's a small world,' she says. 'My family still live there. I visit regularly. Catch The *Spirit,* then a bus down. It's easy.'

It's a small world, for sure; you always find that. I'm convinced that if you decided to have an affair in, say, Iraq or Uzbhekistan, your girlfriend's cousin or the ex-partner of someone you worked with, would see you and report back. She wishes me well for the rest of my trip and we head off in opposite directions, she back to her cows and me, to cross the Batman Bridge and travel up the other side of the valley to Georgetown, Australia's third oldest settlement.

***

Georgetown is presented in the tourist blurb as one of the prettiest Georgian towns in Tassie. It looks a little run down to me, jaded – or maybe it's just off season and in summer it smartens up. The *Bass and Flinders Centre* is marvellous, though. In 1798, mates and explorers, George Bass and Matthew Flinders, were dispatched to Van Diemen's Land to discover, once and for all, whether it was an island. They sailed with a crew of eight in the sloop, *Norfolk.* On their way through Bass Strait, they entered the Tamar River and anchored off what is now Georgetown.

Bern Cuthbertson and a team of volunteers constructed a replica of the *Norfolk* and, in 1998, re-enacted the journey. The *Bass and Flinders Centre* is now the home of the replica, along with the ex-naval cutter, *Kenneth Dickenson,* and a whale boat, rowed around Tasmania by James Kelly, an adventurer from Hobart. The *Norfolk* sits on a platform overseeing the centre and I'm over the moon. Matthew Flinders was one of the idols of my youth, following my reading of *My Love Must Wait*, a rather romanticised biography by Ernestine Hill. The ship is tiny and, recalling the wildness of the coastline at Arthur River, I can't imagine how so many of the larger ships survived, let alone this one.

I follow my heritage map around the town from one old cottage to the next, checking the dates on every plaque and ending at the *Watch House Museum,* originally the local lockup. It's now a craft and information centre and houses a miniature village, a replica of Georgetown as it was when it was established. It's not on the scale of *Old Hobart Town* in Richmond but it still gives me a good idea of how the town was in its early days. In the adjoining rooms is a display of quilt-making. I've never given much thought to quilt-making, labelling it as a sort of 'Jane Austenish' thing little old ladies do to keep themselves occupied. How wrong was I! These are works of art, unbelievably intricate: portraits, scenes, still life's, more like they've been painted than sewn. Sorry, ladies (and men) who make quilts.

I'm booked into a cabin at Low Head, five kilometres north of Georgetown. Low Head is home to Australia's oldest continuously operating pilot station. Although the Tamar River is quite wide, the channel is narrow and contains reefs and rocks and a strong current. All ships bringing supplies to Launceston go through this point to be piloted through to Launceston. The Museum has a fabulous array of maritime memorabilia: barometers, sextants, items from ship wrecks, much of it from the barque, *Asterope,* which was wrecked on Hebe Reef at the mouth of the river, in the 1880s. An early diving suit sits in a corner, along with the compressor that pumped air down into the suit. Weights and heavy boots prevented the incumbent from drifting off with the current. They must have been awfully brave to go underwater in that gear.

A glass case is filled with artefacts found around Low Head. One is shackles from a convict escapee, the seal unbroken. The shackle has been bashed into an oval shape so the prisoner could get his heel through the gap. A wall of photos shows families on holiday. It's not my idea of somewhere to take the kids but perhaps they enjoyed wandering around mud flats. The museum is a maze of rooms and by the time I arrive back at the first, the woman who greeted me has been replaced by a man and I realise it's well past closing time. I apologise but he seems genuinely happy that I've taken such an interest in the displays.

My cabin is small, just a box, really, but with everything I need. The wind whistles across the mud flats as I drag my case through the doorway. Tassie is good for my fitness. I've walked miles today and all I want now is to sleep. Tomorrow I'm looking forward to seeing the beauty of the Tamar Valley on my way back over the Batman Bridge and on into Launceston.

Chapter 10

I open my cabin door to fog. The closer I get to the Batman Bridge, the heavier it becomes. I'm always a little anxious crossing bridges, even on foot – what if the screws holding it together choose that moment to give way – so I'm even less keen driving into a white cloud. So much for seeing the Tamar Valley. I stick to the car in front of me, hoping the driver knows where he's going. Ghostly trees, their branches creating grisly apparitions, materialise and fade back into their white canvas. A car appears from nowhere, startling me, and vanishes. Eerie towns ripple into view, their occupants wraithlike, and waft away. The bends in the road become sharper and I can feel myself descending. I grip the steering wheel even harder.

On the outskirts of Launceston, the fog suddenly lifts. I thank my guide as he disappears along a side road. Two and three-storey Victorian mansions, street after street of them, cling to the sides of almost perpendicular hills. I love beautiful buildings, especially old ones, and I'm caught between staring at them and trying not to go sailing off the very windy road into town.

You have to make decisions too quickly when driving in cities and there's always some bloke waiting to use his horn to tell you how stupid you are. This is easy, though. The West Tamar Highway leads straight into the centre of town so I have no trouble finding my way to my motel in Brisbane Street. The room is like a time capsule, reminding me of a trip I took to America in the late 70s: dark wood laminate, brown and beige mosaic bathroom tiles, a mirror over a built-in desk opposite a queen-sized bed – *and* I've discovered my first electric blanket of the trip. Can't wait for bedtime. A picture window looks out toward City Park and just three or four blocks from that is the mall. By the look of the map I'm within walking distance of everything of interest which is fabulous because, as is normal at this stage of a trip, I'd rather slit my wrists than get back in the car. The *Princess Theatre* is a short walk down the hill, it's Friday and I'm keen to see what's on. I know Tassie has a strong arts scene.

'Sorry,' says the girl, 'nothing. If you'd come last week ... or next.'

The city mall is small and quiet. I'm wondering why it *is* so quiet – there are plenty of people around – when I realise there's none of the thumping music that normally bombards you in shopping precincts. It's as if someone, some marketing guru somewhere, has decided that people won't spend without it, that we have to be pounded into submission. Thumping music completely destroys my decision making processes but maybe it has the opposite effect on the under thirties and, let's face it, they're the ones spending the money. The last of the fog has disappeared, the sun is shining and I head toward the wharf. I'm planning to take a cruise up the Tamar Valley, seeing I missed it coming down. I should get a better view from the river, anyway.

'Cancelled,' says the young woman at King's Wharf, 'not enough customers this time of year.' I compromise with the *Cataract Gorge Cruise*. The gorge extends from the mouth of the South Esk River, a short distance from the wharf, up river for five kilometres to the Trevallyn hydro-electricity dam. The fifty minute cruise will take me into the opening of the gorge and back again, hardly the two and a half hours I had intended but better than nothing. I'm starving and sprint along the quay to find something decent to eat, queue up for an interminable amount of time and sprint back again, to find I'm the only customer.

'I'll wait for the next one.'

'You're sure?' she says. 'We don't mind.' A boat cruise just for me? I wander along the river bank past the children's playground and up the hill to *Penny Royal*, a fun park with replicas of a 19th century gunpowder mill, a cannon foundry and a ten gun sloop-of-war. On the way back, I breathe a sigh of relief to see others waiting. I love boat cruises and so I'm happy to relax back into my own little world and be carried along, sedated by the purr of the engine and the cheerful voice of the tour guide.

***

The afternoon sun is blasting through the window of my room as I close the drapes and drop into a chair with my brochures, to check out where I've been and where I still want to go. It's a terrific place to walk around if you're interested in colonial architecture. I wonder why efforts are no longer made to design buildings as works of art as well as for their functionality. Each building seems to be vying with the next for originality and beauty. The few modern buildings, ugly concrete boxes, contrast sharply with the creations of the past. No doubt it's all to do with money.

A coffee rejuvenates me and I set out through City Park to look for something for dinner. Across the road I spy a Chinese restaurant. I've been aching for a spot of fried rice since I arrived; Tasmania seems extraordinarily Anglo-Saxon. *Closed* says the sign. By the look of it, it's been closed for a while. Back in my room, a brochure is advertising 'Indian Takeaway'. Indians have discovered Tassie then, if not Chinese.

***

Launceston is built completely on hills, so two days of climbing has made up for hours of sitting in the car. Most people in Melbourne live in the suburbs and commute to the city to work or for entertainment and shopping, so it surprises me to see homes right down to the main street. I've walked for miles and my neck is sore from twisting, not wanting to miss one gorgeous mansion.

The area was settled in 1804 when Governor King, afraid that the French might settle in Van Diemen's Land, set up the island's northern military base. By 1827, the town had a population of 2000 and was already shipping wool and wheat from the surrounding districts. In 1852, it was proclaimed a municipality and, a decade later, it opened its own stock exchange. It would have been a good time to live in Launceston. I'm wondering what the rates are like now, if it's expensive to live in one of these houses, this close to the city. All seem to be occupied, even *with* the global economic crisis. I trudge back up the hill, through the park and across to the motel. It's 'Indian' again and an early night, nestled into my electric blanket. Tomorrow – the 'Heritage Highway'.

Chapter 11

The Midland, known on the tourist map as the 'Heritage Highway', is dotted with villages that are supposed to look pretty much as they were when they were established in the 1800s. Manoeuvring the car down the steep hill from the driveway of the motel, I follow the directions. Within minutes I'm in the country. **Sunday Market** says the sign at Evandale.

'This is what I use,' says a woman, behind a table covered in skin products. 'It gets rid of wrinkles. See?' She places a finger underneath each eye, inviting an examination of the area. Her knitted beanie and her parka and jeans are not the usual garb for someone selling cosmetics. These are natural products, though, produced at a local herb farm, in which case she looks perfect for the job. 'I'm 65, you know.' She stops to allow it to sink in. 'Sixty-five.' She doesn't look anything like 65, I have to agree. She leans over and rubs some on my hand. 'What do you think? Beautiful, isn't it?' It is. '*You* should use it.' I'm suddenly aware of my puffy eyes and the patchiness of my skin.

'I know I'm not looking too good today but I've been on the road for a week so I'm a bit tired.' I start describing my drama at Arthur River but she interrupts.

'By yourself?'

'Yes.'

'The only way to go. I've been to Europe on my own.'

'Have you? To Europe? I'm too scared so far.'

'Oh no, you don't have to be scared of Europe. I've been to Italy *nine* times ... *by myself*.'

'Nine times?'

'Yes, I mind houses for people.'

'Mind houses?' I'm sounding like one of those parrots that mimic.

'Lived in Positano for months at a time. Positano, it's gorgeous. Completely safe. You'd love it.'

'What about the language?'

'You pick it up. You have to. Sorry,' she says, 'have to go to the toilet while I've got the chance,' and dashes off. She obviously doesn't see me as a customer. And she's probably right. I don't trust anti-wrinkle creams. When they don't work I feel ripped off and get angry and anger is not good for the skin. Still, it's fabulous to talk to another woman who loves exploring and who doesn't think twice about going it alone. Most people you talk to, at home or on the road, can't believe you'd travel by yourself, as if there's some great danger out there that dissipates if you have a friend with you – or a man. There's a sense that you're breaking some rule, one of those obscure ones that you should automatically understand. This lady seems braver than me, though if she can do it, *why* can't I? Her voice darts across from a stall behind me. I change my mind.

'I'll have this one,' I say, catching her eye. She's disappointed with my choice but pulls back from saying so and proceeds to tell me the difficulty she's having selling her mud brick house.

'It's right at the entrance to Cataract Gorge ... *right* at the entrance.' Having just been to the Gorge, I'm suitably impressed.

'You're kidding!'

'Yep, I paid five hundred.'

'Five hundred grand?'

'Yes, but I've only got this little job and the pension so I can't afford it.' I wonder why she bought it in the first place – and how *did* she get a loan for $500,000? She's obviously one of those people who throw themselves into things and think about them later. She's a reminder that age has nothing whatever to do with how you run your life. I have to get moving. I need plenty of time for the heritage estates around Evandale and Longford.

'Don't forget,' she calls. 'Positano. *Do* it.'

***

Thomas Archer was a giant in the early days of the colony. He arrived in 1811 on the cutter, *Guildford*, with a letter of introduction from his uncle, George Street, editor of the *London Courier*. As always, it's who you know. He worked in various Government positions until, in 1813, he was appointed clerk in charge of stores at Port Dalrymple, now Launceston. In 1816, he became coroner and 18 months later, was appointed magistrate for the territory. Governor Macquarie rewarded him for his hard work with a grant of 800 acres in the rich farming land of the Norfolk Plains. By the time he resigned in 1821, the property had grown to 2000 acres.

He called his estate, *Woolmers*, after a property in his home county of Hertford in England. He expanded his stock of cattle and sheep and by 1826, *Woolmers* had become the largest establishment by an individual in the Australian colonies. His success inspired his father and his three brothers, Joseph, William and Edward, to join him. The Archer brothers knew what they were doing. Within a few years they had built many of the homesteads around the district, including *Panshanger, Northbury, Palmerston* and *Brickendon*.

Thomas was elected to Government in 1826. Later in his career, Lady Jane Franklin, wife of Lieutenant-Governor Sir John Franklin, called him 'the bulk of the Legislative Assembly', alluding not just to his honesty and fair-mindedness, but to his size. When he died of dropsy in 1850, the windows of his bedroom had to be extended to allow his body, too large to fit through the doorway, to be removed.

It's a strange house. The original section reflects Thomas's earlier travels – a New South Wales colonial style bungalow with a wide sweeping sandstone veranda facing out across the South Esk River. His son, Thomas William, died six years before him in 1844, and so the estate passed to his ten-year-old grandson, Thomas Chalmers. It was held in trust while he was sent to England to be educated. While there, he studied European architecture and, on returning home, added an Italianate style extension to the front of the house. The exotic furnishings and design of the front are at total odds with the cosiness and simplicity of the rear. A descendant of the family still lives there so I have to be content with only seeing a small part. Disappointing, but I make up for that by wandering around the outbuildings: the barns, shearing sheds, stables and bakery, trying to imagine what it would have been like to live, isolated, on one of these large, self-sufficient properties.

***

'Sorry about the mess,' says the young woman at the entrance to *Brickendon*'s *Heritage Farm*. The large building is designed to represent a barn. I can't see any mess, other than a few chairs that don't match the rest of the paraphernalia. 'We had a wedding last night and we're still cleaning up.'

'Oh right. You have weddings?'

'Weddings, yes. And some of the guests are staying in our cottages so it's been a busy weekend. Have you been to *Brickendon* before?'

'No.'

'Here's your map of the farm. And when you're finished I'll explain how you get to the gardens and the house.'

When William Archer joined Thomas in 1824, he brought with him 77 merino ewes and 3 rams, a Norman cow and bull, pigs and two stallions. He worked at *Woolmers* before buying 420 acres of his own and establishing *Brickendon*. Early estates would not have survived without the free labour and skills of assigned men and women. By 1820, there were more than 220 offences that could result in transportation, so those starting up businesses in the new colony had no problem acquiring labour. The two estates are within sight of each other and so they shared resources, including their convict servants. *Brickendon*'s wheelwright, Benjamin Cooper made and repaired carts for Thomas, James Jones made shoes for the *Woolmers*' men and James Gillin carted *Brickendon*'s wheat to *Woolmers*' mill and brought flour back.

Convicts were expected to work hard but, unlike many other estates, the brothers treated theirs fairly, even at times, generously. I guess the prisoners realised they were on a good thing. They caused little trouble, other than the odd refusal to obey orders or occasional bouts of drunkenness, usually on Sundays when they preferred drinking to attending to their spiritual welfare in the chapel.

I wander from the barns to the granary, the smokehouse to the stables. William preferred to live near his workers and so his original cottage is a short walk from the convict barracks. It was very basic living, just two rooms, but I get the impression William was happy being one of the boys.

'Sorry to keep you,' says the young woman, rushing through a door at the back. 'What did you think of it?'

'It's wonderful,' I say. 'You can almost feel like you're back there in the middle of it.'

'Well, it's a working farm, so you are really in the middle of it.'

'No convicts, though.'

'Now, here is your map of the gardens. You can't go into the house, of course, because the family still lives there. Turn right out of the car park, then left. That will take you into the property.'

I could be in England as I drive along a lane bordered by fences of hawthorn hedges. In 1828, with the idea of marrying, William began building his Georgian mansion, realising, no doubt, that a wife would not want to live next door to convicted criminals. He separated it even further with six hectares of garden. As soon as it was finished he married Caroline Harrison. He was 40, she was 24.

A small white house with a peaked tin roof, a white chimney sprouting from each side, sits invitingly, irresistibly, on one side of the driveway. The green picket fence is bordered by rose bushes and African daisies. It's the original coachman's cottage. There's no-one around and I push through the side gate. My nose is pressed to the back window when a car pulls into the driveway.

'Can I help you?' says a woman. A familiar feeling ripples through me, childhood guilt at being caught out breaking some rule.

'Sorry. I couldn't resist trying to see inside.'

'Would you like a look inside?'

'I *love* to.'

'I look after the accommodation. We had people staying last night and I'm just putting everything back in order.' She juggles the key for a few moments and I enter a small sitting room. A latticed window is painted in a deep blue and framed by white drapes hung from a brass rod. The blue continues around the wall to the fireplace, over which hangs a landscape in an antique burnt gold frame. Burgundy and gold offset the blue in the plump couches and cushions, the table cloth and a large rug. It's very cosy, very much the real thing, though I can't help thinking the couches could do with a re-upholster. She must have read my mind.

'We've left it pretty much as it would have been,' she says. 'People want that feeling of 'old'.' Of course they do. Having new couches would destroy that. 'This was the coachman's office,' she says, as we pass through a small, dark room and into the kitchen. This has definitely been renovated – no contemporary person would want to cook their dinner in a pot over the fireplace. The back wall has been replaced by more modern latticed glass doors. The sunlight pours through as I look out to the pretty yard, with its longish grass and its garden of daisies, geraniums and lavender. The stairs to the second floor are incredibly steep and narrow. I wonder how many children catapulted down these before working them out. Upstairs are two large bedrooms.

'It's surprisingly big,' I say to the woman, as she drops some towels onto the bed.

'Yes. The coachman was the most senior of the servants, so he had the largest cottage. He was responsible for the horses and carriages, all important, of course, at the time. He had to have them ready to go at a moment's notice.' She pats the bedspreads and adjusts a lace curtain. 'I have to get moving. I've got others to check before I finish.'

'That was good timing,' I say, as I pick my way down the tiny staircase. 'I don't usually get any further than peering through windows.' She locks the door, waves and takes off up the road.

The main house is designed with a central block and two double-storey wings. A wall and gates form a fourth side, enclosing a court yard, where staff and livestock could take refuge from bushrangers – or Aborigines peeved at having their families killed by smoking fire sticks and their land destroyed by strange woolly creatures. I'm devastated there's no access to the house. Most estates let you have at least a peek. A pathway lined with rose bushes leads to the orchard where sheep are grazing. It's very quiet, except for the chatter of a toddler and his parents somewhere close by but out of sight in the gardens. Across the hills, in the distance, is *Woolmers*. It would have been a comfort, I imagine, for the families to be able to look across the hills and see each others' homes. The short trip between the two must have allayed some of the loneliness; that is, if they got on. The brothers definitely did – the wives, I have no idea.

Chapter 12

An avenue of elm trees creates a theatrical introduction to Ross. The road is flanked by original stone cottages and stores. If I was in a carriage rather than a car, I could easily imagine myself back in the first half of the 19th century. The area had been under military guard since 1812, to protect travellers and local settlers from the ever-present bushrangers. In 1821, Governor Macquarie passed through, naming the river after himself, and recorded in his journal: "I named our last night's station, Ross, in honour of H. M. Buchanan Esq, that being the name of his seat on Loch Lomond in Scotland; this part of Argyle Plains on the right bank of the Macquarie River being very beautiful and commanding a noble view." Later that year, a timber bridge was built over the river and Ross became an important stopover between Launceston and Hobart.

I stop in at the bakery. The little dining room is almost full. The warmth of the log fire and the yellow walls add to the already cheerful atmosphere. I order coffee and a huge vanilla slice, trying not to think about the diet I'll need by the time I get home. I follow my heritage map from one site to another, hoping that will negate the effects of the vanilla slice, beginning at the crossroads at the centre of town. These are referred as the 'Four Corners of Ross', each corner having a label: Temptation – *Man O' Ross Hotel*; Recreation – *Town Hall*; Salvation – *Catholic Church*; Damnation – *Gaol*.

The *Ross Female Factory* is now just a stone wall, along with the cottage that was the original staff quarters. It was designed as a facility for transferring female convicts to and from private service. According to Comptroller-General Hampton: "Women long resident in Launceston and Hobart, who have formed numerous vicious associations in these towns, can now be forced to remain in the rural districts, in circumstances of less temptation and with stronger incentives to well doing." He was probably right. It would certainly have been healthier than other prisons around the colony, which were built entirely of stone and were damp all year round. The women tended a large garden, cared for livestock, chopped firewood and carried water.

Still, in many cases the women would have been in less danger if not put in the factories in the first place. Many of the staff were as corrupt as the inmates. Forms of contraband and currency passed between the two. There were numerous pregnancies at Ross, even though men were supposedly banned. Superintendent, N. J. Irvine, was particularly worried about lesbianism. In 1850, he wrote to Robert Stuart, a visiting magistrate: "I proceed to lay before you some few particulars respecting the unnatural practices ... amongst female convicts; these women may be naturally divided into female and pseudo-males ... whose presence is particularly sought out, and every inducement offered to them to join company with those addicted to these depraved and abominable habits; the first class ... are habitually in the practice of making numerous presents to their 'lovers' so that an individual who acts the infamous part of the pseudo-male, is most comfortably provided for ... with every procurable luxury. The young and comparatively innocent class of female convicts appear to be those on whom the unenviable choice of the pseudo-male is fixed, and a large proportion of the juvenile female convicts are, to use the words of one informant, by these means ... ruined."

I drive out to the Old Cemetery, to see if I can locate the burial spot of stonemason, Daniel Herbert. He was transported in 1827 for highway robbery – obviously, not a lot of work around, at the time, for stonemasons. Herbert, along with another stonemason, James Colbert, oversaw the construction of the Ross Bridge. The bridge was commissioned by Governor Arthur and designed by John Lee Archer. Built by convicts in local sandstone, it's the third oldest bridge still in use in Australia. Herbert crafted 186 carvings to decorate the three arches of the bridge. These include animals and plants, Celtic symbols, faces of local identities and, no doubt as a political expedient, the dial of Governor Arthur. He was even able to slip in his own likeness, along with that of his wife. The Roman Numerals, *MDCCCXXXVI*, represents 1836, the year the bridge was completed.

In 1842, in acknowledgement of his work on the bridge and many sites around Hobart, Herbert was granted a full pardon and lived out the rest of his life in Ross, working as an ornamental stonemason. He died of pneumonia on 28th February, 1868. Reputedly, he designed and carved his own tomb and here I am standing in front of it. A tablet on four thick, octagonal-shaped legs supports a beautiful urn, looking a bit like a genii's lamp without the spout and handle. The inscription is simple: *Daniel Herbert Died Feb 28th 1868 Aged 68 Years.* I have a feeling that Daniel is at peace here, looking out toward his beautiful bridge. Meanwhile, the carvings are now 173 years old and slowly eroding. Investigations are underway as to the best way to preserve them. They may have to be removed and replaced by replicas. *That* would be sad. Currently, the pieces have been treated with a silicose spray to slow down the erosion process.

The lighting in the *Tasmanian Wool Centre* is dim but not dim enough to hide the prices on the stunning woollen products. I steer myself away, back out into the sunshine to continue my explorations. Next stop, Oatlands.

***

Ever since organising this trip I've been waiting to spend Sunday night in what is, from the photo on its website, a beautiful heritage hotel in Oatlands. Perhaps it's because it's nearly dark and difficult to see, that the hotel doesn't look that beautiful. The girl behind the bar eyes me suspiciously.

'I'm booked in here tonight,' I say.

'Oh, okay.' She refills a beer glass then disappears up a passage. Three men hunch over the bar and several others lounge at a table. The conversation lagged when I entered, a frequent experience of mine. They don't expect women 'of an age' and as conservative looking as me, to be in a pub. The lighting's bad but I can tell this room hasn't had a paint job or maintenance in centuries. I don't think I've ever seen anything quite as messy as the back of the bar. It reminds me of a garage where mates meet up to get away from their wives, have a beer and talk sport – one of those spots they use to store things they can't throw out in case they'll come in handy some time. This is not what I was expecting. I could escape now, no-one would care but it's too late to start looking for somewhere else. I learnt that on my last trip. You don't go out into the dark in Tasmania without somewhere to stay. You could end up spending the whole night on the road. I'll take my chances here.

The room is a surprise, large, with a double bed and electric blanket, television and heater. 'Where's the bathroom,' I ask, hoping it's not too far away. She opens the door to an en suite. A shower revives me and I'm suddenly starving. I'm looking forward to a nice meal and a glass of red in the bistro.

'Not open Sundays,' says the girl. 'The kitchen's round there. They'll make you something.'

'I was sent in here by the girl at the bar,' I say to the woman in the kitchen.

'Yeah? Whad d' you want?'

'Umm.'

'I can cook you whatever,' she says. 'Steak, sausages?'

'Is it just me? Won't it put you out?' She looks at me as if I've just arrived from a planet far, far away.

'I've just done ten for the workers.' Workers? What workers? I'm out of my comfort zone as it is, ordering food; I never got the hang of it – comes from growing up in the bush and not having entered a cafe until my late teens – and so my mind goes completely blank.

'Here,' she says, stuffing a menu in my hand, 'let me know,' and vanishes. Scrambled eggs and bacon sounds easy but now I can't find her. A teenage boy wanders past me into the kitchen with a dirty dinner plate and fades back to wherever he came from. I ask the girl at the bar what they have in reds. She looks disconcerted, as if I've asked something difficult.

'Umm ... we've got this.' She holds up a half-empty bottle of *Sacred Hill*.

'Right. I'll have a vodka and orange.' The drink comes in a beer glass. Obviously not a lot of spirits drinkers in Oatlands. I grab the cook as she passes and order my eggs and bacon.

It's actually quite pleasant sitting on a couch in front of the log fire, though even in my *Millers*' shirt, I'm overdressed. A very drunk man lurches from behind me, alternately talking to himself and singing, and drops onto one of the other couches. He stares at a newspaper, keeping up his discourse the whole time. I feel sorry for him; I understand his need for filling the silence with sounds, keeping any possibility of disturbing thoughts away. After ten minutes he staggers out again, chattering all the way. There's a kindness here, allowing someone so needy to be part of the furniture.

I eat my meal from the coffee table, leave my glass on the bar and return to my room. Men thump at intervals up the stairs and along the passage. I'm not totally convinced this is your average hotel. I check that my door is locked, just in case I get a visitor in the middle of the night expecting extra-curricular activities.

***

One of the things I like about staying in pubs is that breakfast is included in the price. I pour some cereal and set myself up in front of the still burning fire to study my map. I'm heading down to the Tasman Peninsula and Port Arthur. A small cafe area that I didn't notice last night takes up one end of the room, and two chattering women appear and start preparing to open it. They are chic, efficient and the deli could fit in anywhere in Melbourne. By the time I'm ready to leave they're serving breakfasts. The hotel has two lives: a night-time one which services workmen, probably the ones that keep holding me up on the roads – there are road works everywhere – and a daytime one, servicing the town and passing traffic. It's been a weird and interesting experience.

***

Oatlands began life as a military base, from where convicts were assigned work on farms, public buildings, roads and bridges. It was named by Governor Macquarie, and through the 1820s, became home to farmers, convicts and bushrangers. One of its most famous residents was Solomon Blay, ex-convict and Tasmania's most feared hangman. Blay, needless to say, was the most unpopular public servant in Van Diemen's Land. As well as Oatlands, he had to ply his trade at Richmond, and as far away as Launceston and Hobart. His wages were so low that he couldn't afford a horse and he was so reviled that no stage coach would pick him up. He had to tramp, swag on his back, sometimes taking three days to get from one place to another. It's a harsh way to treat someone. After all, he was only doing his job; someone had to do it. Oatlands is a pretty place, sedate now, compared with what I imagine would have been a pretty wild and woolly past. I do a quick circuit, lingering at the Callington Mill, built in 1837 and about to be restored, no doubt to help in the fiercely competitive world of the tourist dollar.

Chapter 13

Ever since reading, *For the Term of His Natural Life*, by Marcus Clarke, I've wanted to visit Eaglehawk Neck, the narrow isthmus, a mere 30 metres wide, at the top of The Tasman Peninsula. The Neck is the only way through by land from *Port Arthur Penal Settlement* to the rest of the island. Governor Arthur posted a guard station there to prevent escapees from Port Arthur getting any further. Still, escapes continued, as Eaglehawk Neck is dotted with sandy hummocks which give cover and the surf blots out the sound of footsteps.

To put a stop to them, the ensign in charge of the guard, Irishman, Captain John Peyton Jones, had the bright idea of chaining up a line of vicious dogs, which went ballistic at the tiniest sound or movement. In the quiet, shallow waters on the west side, he placed three platforms on poles and installed dogs on them, to give the alarm if a 'bolter' tried to wade across. Legend has it that offal and blood, from the slaughtering station further up the coast, were dumped, to draw sharks. This may have been true or maybe that's just what they told the convicts.

In 1840, Henry Melville, editor of Hobart's *Colonial Times*, described the dogs thus: "Those out of the way pretenders to dogship rejoiced in such soubriquets as Caesar, Pompey, Ajax, Archilles, Ugly Mug, Jowler, Tear'em and Muzzle'em. There were the black, the white, the brindle, the grey and the grisly, the rough and the smooth, the crop-eared and the lop-eared, the gaunt and the grim. Every four-footed, black-fanged individual among them would have taken first prize in his own class for ugliness and ferocity at any show." I'd be fierce if I was chained to a platform in the middle of the sea (not to mention being brutally insulted for my less than perfect looks).

Still, as at *Sarah Island*, many still tried. One character, a former actor named William Hunt, disguised himself as a kangaroo and attempted to hop across the Neck. The soldiers were shocked when, as one of them raised his musket to shoot the 'large boomer', the animal threw up his hands and gave himself up. Now *that* would have been something to talk about over a pint. I attempt the crossing, *sans* vicious dogs, but the walkway is flooded and so I miss out.

The military station was established in 1831, with an officer, a sergeant and 25 soldiers and their wives. A store and jetty accompanied the officers' quarters and military barracks and a hut served as a schoolroom for the children. To warn of escapes and crises in *Port Arthur* and to receive messages from Hobart, commandant, Charles O'Hara Booth, set up a chain of signal stations, a 'telegraph' without electricity. It was run by semaphores, tall poles set on hilltops and islands, each carrying three sets of double arms, like railway signals. By a system of chains, each arm could be set at various angles, and each angle was allotted a numerical meaning. The number-groups translated into words, phrases and whole sentences through a code book. Booth spent years on his signal book, and by 1844 it listed 11,300 signals, sent through a network of 22 stations. News of a 'bolter' could flash from Port Arthur to Eaglehawk Neck in one minute flat.

Still, it didn't always work. Booth wrote in his code book: "Should it occur that a signal cannot pass from the badness of the weather or should prisoners abscond during the night, much time may be gained by a soldier or a constable being despatched to the head of the railroad and discharging two shots, one quickly succeeding the other, which will be passed on in a similar manner, that is, by firing a double shot from station to station, until it arrives at Eaglehawk Neck, when the sentinel on the jetty will answer it in the same manner and immediately report the circumstances." Simple, but eminently effective.

Booth obviously had a lot of time on his hands or else he was seriously hyperactive. Apart from establishing a coal mine on the western side of Norfolk Bay, he developed a railway that connected the dock of Norfolk Bay, near Eaglehawk Neck, to Port Arthur, some four and a half miles away. It had no engine and was powered by convicts, trotting and pushing against crossbars at the front and rear. Colonel Godfrey Mundy, a visitor to Port Arthur in 1851, wrote: "when getting up steam, down they rattled at tremendous speed ... the chains around their ankles clinking and clanking as they trotted along ... the runners jumped upon the side of the trucks in rather unpleasant proximity with the passengers, and away we all went, bondsmen and freemen, jolting and swaying ... a man sitting behind contrived, more or less, to lock a wheel with a wooden crowbar when the descent became so rapid as to call for remonstrance."

The trucks could reach 30 miles per hour, pretty terrifying for ladies who were used to going no faster than a trotting horse. Still, I'm sure there were some adventurous types who saw it as a short but exhilarating escape from their corseted, repressed lives. Lieutenant-Governor William Denison rode a similar railway at Ralph Bay Neck and gave another version: "I must say that my feelings at seeing myself seated and pushed along by these miserable convicts, were not very pleasant. It was painful to see them in the condition of slaves, which, in fact, they were, waiting for me up to their knees in water."

Further south, the ocean has battered the 300 metre high, dolomite cliffs for millennia, creating monumental rock formations, flutes, gigantic stacks and spectacular pillars. It's drizzling as I lean over the railing at the huge archway named after Abel Tasman. The ground vibrates, echoing through me, as the furious waves pound at the base of the arch, wearing it away inch by inch. I meander along to The *Blowhole*, an unusual formation, carved by the sea through the sheer rock face, creating a tunnel through which periodic ruptures of water can spurt up to 10 metres high. The rain eases and I stand for a while, hypnotised, as the water squeezes its way through, explodes in anger on discovering it is trapped, and works its way out again.

***

A sign hangs on a garage at the cabin park at Murdunna, just south of Dunalley: **Reception**. If **Reception** is a garage, I'm wondering what the rest of the place is like, but the studio cabin is almost new.

'Sorry about the grounds,' says my host, Harvey, 'but we've had more rain in the last two months than we normally get for the whole year.'

'Really?'

'Yep. July is usually sunny with very little wind.'

'Really?' I'm doing that parrot thing again.

'There's milk in the fridge and bread and butter and a toaster for your breakfast. Did you see the hotel on your way through?'

'I did.' I'm still getting over the surprise of it; an enormous clinker-brick hotel, framed by wide verandas, gabled windows jutting from its first floor and tall chimneys sprouting from its grey iron roof, seemingly in the middle of nowhere. There must be more people around here than I thought.

'I can recommend the food. That's where most of our guests go.'

'Thanks.'

'Right, I'll leave you to it, then.'

It's an unusual park, just six cabins set in a semi-circle: no playground, swimming pool or facilities for caravans. They're definitely not encouraging families, which is fine by me. I'm not averse to children – our family has its fair share of them – but I'm just as happy with the peace and quiet I'm expecting from this backwater. Looking through the glass sliding door I can just see, through some tall shrubs, the top of Mt. Wellington. I'd like to check out my surroundings but it's started raining again so, for the moment, I'm opting for shelter.

***

It's interesting to me the things that people don't consider when designing cabins. There's always some simple arrangement that could be made to make them work better and I wonder why it's not thought of at the time. In the studio cabin at Arthur River the bathroom is massive, and yet there's not one shelf to put toiletries on. I could have put the toilet lid down and used that, except that the toilet is on the other side of the room, much too far away to be of any use. As well, the mirror is on a different wall to the sink and I wonder how men manage shaving. Doesn't make applying makeup easier, either. Here, there's no kitchen, which is fine, except that the jug has to be filled at the bathroom sink, but the tap is too low for the jug to fit under. I resort to holding it under the shower, wishing I had someone to take a photo. It would make a good holiday snap.

Sitting up in bed with a book, the heater on and every blanket I can find, I relax at last and all is well with the world. I'd like to stay here for a break but I'm booked in tomorrow night at White Beach, closer to Port Arthur. It's hard to believe I have only two nights left before returning to Devonport for the trip home. The first few days seemed to take forever and now the last are going so quickly I can't keep a hold of them.

***

It's 8am, the rain has stopped and I don my beanie and scarf and pick my way through the puddles and mud, down a pathway in the scrub and onto a half-moon beach of white sand. Headlands reach toward each other at either end, the blue layers of their hills graduating to a deep purple in the distance. In the centre, as if placed there by a landscape designer, is Mt. Wellington. I'm the only one taking advantage of this stunning scene. I guess the locals have become accustomed to it – or else they have more sense than to brave the piercing wind at this time of the morning.

***

I have little memory of *Port Arthur* from when I came years ago. My companion booked me onto a bus tour without asking if I was interested and so I'd started out in a bad frame of mind. I had preconceptions from pictures I'd seen in history books, and the scene I arrived at didn't match those. I'd imagined it to have been less tidy, somehow, less manicured.

In 1827, the brig, *Opossum*, returned from a trip between Maria Island and Hobart, with news of a deep, sheltered inlet, surrounded by colossal stands of timber. Governor Arthur had been looking for somewhere closer to Hobart to replace *Sarah Island*. He sent a surveyor to make a detailed report on its merits as a port, its water supply and, above all, its forests. Logging would have the dual purpose of creating work for the convicts and filling the ever-rising demand for timber for buildings and furniture.

The first group of 34 new English prisoners and 15 soldiers under the command of Dr. John Russell, arrived in 1830, along with a group of convicts from *Sarah Island*. Rations were miserably short, scurvy widespread and medical supplies almost non-existent. Russell's pleas for aid went unheard as Arthur's attention had drifted away to his latest obsession – rounding up what was left of the island's black tribes. Charles O'Hara Booth was appointed in 1833 to pull the settlement into shape. In the next decade, manufacturing such as ship building, shoemaking, smithing and brick making was established. A thriving township developed and continued to expand as convicts pushed further into the encircling hills to extract the valuable timber.

Port Arthur has had bad press over the years, represented as the hell hole of all hell holes. In fact, it was run on a minute code of government regulations, which prevented the sadism that was rife in early settlements such as Macquarie Harbour and Norfolk Island. Still, it wasn't somewhere you'd choose to go for a quiet weekend. Arthur's instructions were: "The most unceasing labour is to be exacted from the convicts and the most harassing vigilance over them is to be observed." The sequence of offence, detection and punishment had such a machine-like regularity, that the men were consigned to a sort of bovine existence, Arthur's idea of reformation. Booth preferred the use of solitary confinement to the lash, because the lash "often exasperates them and drives them to crime instead of reforming them," whereas solitary confinement was "much dreaded ... subdues them through boredom."

I wonder how the free settlers felt about living next door to a prison, and about some of the treatment meted out to the more difficult inmates. The odd scream must have been carried by the wind, or a moan from a long-termer gone mad. In 1996, Martin Bryant, a 28 year old from New Town, a suburb of Hobart, killed 35 people and wounded 21 others in and around the *Port Arthur* site. When asked why he chose that spot he answered that "a lot of violence had happened there, it must be the most violent place in Australia; it seemed the right place."

I was anxious about coming back for this reason, worried that the deeds of that day still hung in the air. Could some residue of Bryant's actions have remained because it was "the right place" for them or had it been blown out to sea by the wind, swallowed up by the trees and dispersed by prayers? A large visitor centre has been built to replace the smaller Broad Arrow cafe where a lot of the murders took place. A memorial sits quietly along a pathway. It's understated, respectful and surprisingly calming.

I spend four and a half hours following my map from one site to another. Many of the original buildings were destroyed in the bush fires of 1895 and 1897 – the penitentiary and the hospital are now shells, allowing light into what must have been icy cold and soul-destroying darkness. I take the short boat trip out to Point Puer, an island that housed boys between nine and 18 who were caught up in the mechanisms of British law. These boys were a dead weight on the British Government, which decided to off-load them onto Governor Arthur, with the idea of having them trained in useful employment. They were kept at Point Puer away from the influence of the older men, but most of them had already spent months or years in prisons and on ships with adults, so it was a bit late, to say the least.

By 1842, there were 716 inmates on the island, along with a jumble of barracks, workrooms and schoolrooms.

Booth followed Arthur's instructions to treat the boys pretty much like the adults, starting their days at 5am and working them into the ground so they had no energy for anything else. There's no doubt they received a better education than they would have at home but only in trades that would make them useful as assigned servants. Arthur saw little need for intellectual schooling and even after two or three years in the settlement, some boys had difficulty reading words of one syllable.

It's a horrible thought, the picture of these children, freezing in their little uniforms, picked on by the older boys in the hierarchy that always develops. There were hierarchies elsewhere, as well. Soldiers' wives were used as domestic servants, banned from mixing with the wives of the next level up, and so on up the scale. Normal life, except based around a prison. Some of these girls must have had second thoughts about their decision to marry as they sailed into the harbour of this wild land.

The food and coffee at the Asylum cafeteria is bad, really bad. They call what I'm eating a sausage roll. I'll take their word for it. Apart from the food, *Port Arthur* is brilliant.

Chapter 14

I'm at the holiday park at White Beach. It's empty. I have to say, if you want peace and quiet, the middle of winter is definitely the time to come to Tassie. The only trouble is that parks are left in charge of caretakers and they don't seem to have much of a handle on the job.

'I've put you in a different cabin,' the woman says, pleased with herself, 'to catch some afternoon sun.' It's very nice of her to be so thoughtful, except that I don't think this cabin was prepared for visitors. Every little disposable packet of milk is off and I'm desperate for coffee, having been unable to finish the one at *Port Arthur*.

'All of them off?' says the woman, 'I'm not sure if we've got any more.' I wait while she rattles around in a back room. 'Yep, there you are.' She drops a half dozen on the counter. 'Have those.'

I open one after the other. They're all gone, so it looks like no tea or coffee, and canned fruit for breakfast. The floor's not too clean. I'm not one for keeping up with housework myself but that's at home and it's my dirt. I'm not keen on others'.

'There's no heater,' I tell the woman.

'The air-conditioner is two-way.'

I can't get it to work, there are no instructions and I'm not facing her again, just in case it's me and not the air-conditioner. The can opener's broken and the batteries in the television remote are dead. The only thing to do when nothing works is to go to bed. An early night is in order, anyway. I'm booked in, tomorrow, for a boat cruise around Tasman Island. I'm determined to get a taste of nature, seeing I've been deprived of forests, and I'm really looking forward to it.

***

I *was* really looking forward to it but at this moment I'm wondering whether I should just slither over the side and put an end to my misery. Because it's years since I've been on the water, other than boats that do five kilometres an hour up rivers, I'd forgotten how sea-sick I get. In fact, I get sick on all forms of transport, except, for some odd reason, trains. I felt queasy on the bus that brought us down to the dock as it rocketed around the hills. The conversation between the driver and one of the other passengers on just how dicey it was on these narrow roads and how one lapse in concentration could send us over the edge, was not helpful.

Ginger tablets were handed out as we were leaving the dock, a bit late to say the least but I accepted them without pointing this out. Tablets need to be taken well in advance of the trip and anyway ginger doesn't work for hopeless cases like me. I got seasick coming back from the Barrier Reef. I desperately want to see the cliffs and the seals and the lighthouse and get the full experience of the wildness of this area but it's awfully hard with your head in a bucket.

'How're you goin' now, mate?' The skipper puts his arm around my shoulder. He's taken off my beanie and scarf and put them aside. 'You have to stay cool. Open your coat.' This is his third trip around to see how I'm faring. 'I know exactly how you feel. I worked on fishing boats where you're out for days at a time.'

'I'm devastated,' I blurt out, 'I really wanted photos but I just can't manage it.' He offers to do it for me till I remember the camera batteries are flat. He'd make a fantastic mother; I've never felt so cared for.

And so here I am, in minus something degrees, with the wind from the southern ocean blasting through me. You know you're really sick when you don't care what anyone thinks of you – which is lucky when you're making sounds you wouldn't want your mother to hear. The couple I was sitting with have moved, discreetly, to the other side of the boat. Periodically, I lift my head to look at what's being pointed out, then quickly drop it back to safety.

Tasman Lighthouse is mind blowing. I can't comprehend how anyone could scale the sheer, rocky cliffs, let alone build a lighthouse at the top. Understandably, because of its isolation, it was extremely unpopular with all the light keepers and, I assume, their wives. You'd have to be awfully keen on your man to live up there. It was built in 1906. Stores and goods had to be transferred from a steamer onto a launch and then to a flying fox, which took it to a ledge on the island about 100 feet above the sea. From there the goods were hauled by an engine-driven winch along a tramline up the cliff to around 700 feet, and then to a horse-drawn tramway for the final part of the journey. Too bad if you left something off your list – or changed your mind about what you wanted for dinner.

The basket holding the goods also carried human beings, something I can't even think about without having to hold onto the nearest seat to allay vertigo. On one occasion the door failed to close and a 90-year-old Mrs. Jacobs spent the trip half in and half out, held onto grimly by one of the luckier passengers inside. Undeterred, she made further visits to the island. That's taking family commitment to a whole new level.

Tasman Island was originally thickly forested but was gradually denuded by the cutting of the trees for fuel. Eventually, there was nothing to stop the ferocious wind from causing continual damage to the tower and the buildings, and the fences around them. Repairing the tower must have been terrifying. In 1924, the Lighthouse Service installed their version of a fire escape: a length of rope fitted with a spring hook which could be clipped to the balcony to, I assume, allow those trapped, to climb down the outside. I think I'd rather take my chances with the fire – or just throw myself over and end it quickly. In 1976, the lighthouse was automated and is now solar-powered.

I've come to dread stopping, as the boat heaves backwards and forwards and I heave with it. I wonder why, out of the 30 or so adults and children, I'm the only one that's sick. 'Be over soon,' says the skipper, on his next time around. 'We're on the home run.' He's been saying that for ages and I no longer believe him. 'Okay, everyone,' he says, pointing, 'we'll head through this gap.

We make it most times.' Before anyone has time to think about what he's just said, the driver puts his foot on the accelerator, we turn on our side and shoot through the narrow gap between a great pointed monolith and the cliff. *Tasman Island Cruises* have turned a boat trip into an adventure.

'How are ya, mate? You okay now?' he says, as I step gingerly onto the pier. I thank him for his thoughtfulness. 'No worries, mate.' I'm joined by the couple that had removed themselves to the other side of the boat, as I trudge up the hill that leads back to the company office.

'I spent eight hours on a fishing boat once,' the man says, 'and I was sick the whole time. I thought I was going to die. I reckon it took a week to get over it.' He looks at his wife. 'Didn't it?' She nods. As usual, my stomach started recovering the minute I hit solid ground. I'm exhausted and a little embarrassed now that I feel better.

'Will you be alright?' the woman asks, as we reach the top of the hill. I'm on my own and she's worried for me.

'I'll be fine,' I say. 'I'm okay now.' They wave goodbye.

A knock on the car window startles me. 'There y'are,' says the skipper, handing me some postcards, 'to make up for the photos you missed out on.' He leaves before I have time to thank him. I move the car to a restaurant across the road. A couple stare at me as I enter and sit down. They were on the boat and I interpret their looks as compassion, though maybe they're grimacing. It's hard to tell.

'Sorry to disturb you,' says a nervous voice. It's the woman who walked me up the hill. 'We've just stayed at an absolutely beautiful 'Bed and Breakfast', and they look after you so well and it's cheap at the moment and I just thought you might like to know about it.' She wants me taken care of and I'm incredibly moved.

'I've got to keep moving upwards,' I say. 'I'm heading back tomorrow.' She rushes off, embarrassed that she may have been sticking her nose in where it wasn't wanted. The thoughtfulness I've received today has made the experience almost worth the discomfort. If, as people often say, no-one cares about anyone any more, they need to come to the south of Tassie. And I did glimpse the magnificent scenery, enough to remember anyway and to re-experience with my postcards.

***

'Thanks for coming back,' says Harvey, at the cabin park at Murdunna.

'I was going to be much further up the Midland,' I say, 'but I got terribly seasick today and I'm still recovering.' I'm looking for a bit of sympathy but he's heard it all before and escapes. I drag my stuff from the car and flop onto the bed. Lying here, in this comfortable little cabin, there's a feeling of having come home. A glow issues through the window. The sunset has turned the sky crimson. I throw on my runners and dash through the mud to the beach. The colour reflects off the ocean, the red gradually morphing through shades of pink, ending in a soft rose beneath Mt. Wellington. It fades quickly into darkness and a million stars ornament the sky. My dinner is toast and cold baked beans.

***

I'm up and packed early to allow some time to explore the beach in daylight. I want to fix the scene in my memory, to be sure of taking it home with me. I'm always anxious about time on the last day, worried something awful will happen, an accident or a car breakdown, causing me to miss the boat. I stop again at the bakery at Ross for a coffee and cake. Just the other side of town I'm pulled up by a policeman and a detour sign.

'Roadworks?' I ask.

'Bad accident,' he says. 'Two people killed.' *That's* something I didn't want to know.

They say if you want to make God laugh, tell him your plans. He must be on the floor by now as I wind around a back road, going I don't know where. Luckily it's still morning – I have loads of time. I stop to consult my map. A car passes me, begins to reverse, then takes off again when she sees me pull out. There is no doubt she was a local, checking to see if the detour had caused me to become lost. Again I feel cared for in Tassie. It's a very pretty drive through the countryside and I'm heading in the right direction, so I sit back and enjoy being somewhere I haven't been before. It's funny how things happen. If I hadn't stopped for coffee in Ross I could have been right in the middle of that accident.

***

My intention was to have a really good look around Devonport but getting here early afternoon I realise I did it last time. It's an easy place to forget. After all, *Katies*, *Target*, *Subway*, look the same everywhere. I'm interested in seeing *Home Hill*, the former home of Joseph and

Edith Lyons, but it's closed for winter. A pleasant Italian coffee shop helps pass some time and I drive to the beach, read for awhile and join the queue at the dock for the trip home.

In the bar, I order a red wine and chat to, or more truthfully, earbash, a woman on my ordeal of trying to stick to my plans against all the odds. The man next to me moves away. Maybe I've irritated him. It's amazing how important and dramatic your own travels seem compared with others'. My adventures echo in my head and pour out of their own accord, Arthur River in particular, missing the boat cruise and the Tarkine – the reasons I came in the first place – and the storm. People drift away and others take their places but they're closed off and so I head to the stern of the ship to wait out the night.

October 2009

Chapter 15

The ship is lit up like a fairy palace as I sit in the queue waiting to board. I'm retracing the steps I took in July, three months ago, and this time I intend to see what I missed out on. It's Spring and all tourist attractions will be open, including river cruises. Arthur River's winter storms should be well over. The car has been checked by my *Nissan* dealership and passed as perfect, and so I'm not expecting any coughing, wheezing or complaining on gravel roads. Even pot holes will be taken in its stride.

I have again booked a 'luxury' recliner, but this time I'm going to be comfortable. I've brought a small case to rest my feet on, as suggested by the woman at the Sunday market at Evandale. This will prevent back ache, caused by my short legs dangling six inches above the floor. A movie will get me through till midnight and two herbal sedatives will take me peacefully through till morning, oblivious to the snores and variable night noises from the bodies around me. I won't hear the humming of the great engines, something you get when you pay less and end up at the stern of the ship, or the comings and goings to the toilets. I will sleep well and wake fresh as a daisy to get on with my adventure.

The buffet is as warm and welcoming as usual and the ship feels like an old friend. A woman and her adult son sit opposite me. They are from somewhere in northern Victoria, that's all I can get out of them, and so I take the hint and leave them alone, order a wine and set myself up in front of a television screen to wait out the two hours till the movie starts.

The cinema is empty, except for a young couple, obviously not there for the movie. I twiddle my thumbs for ten minutes, wondering why nothing's happening on the screen. A family enters and the three children spend five minutes deciding where they'll sit before settling down to fill their faces with sleep-destroying junk food. It *is* the worst movie I've ever spent a half an hour in front of.

Back in the lounge, the lights are dim and the backpackers are already asleep. I take my herbs and settle down for the night. It's midnight and I'm dozing as a man levers himself into the seat in front of me. He plunges it back as far as it can go, causing me to whip my case out of the way just in time to prevent spending the rest of my life with a limp, and goes instantly to sleep. There's just enough space between his seat and mine for me to breathe, *if* the breaths are not too deep. Others wander in, arrange and rearrange themselves, duel with the levers trying to force foot rests up further. 'It's not working,' hisses a man to his wife. I want to enlighten him but he's too far away.

The snores start up but at this stage they're just murmurs and I drift back to sleep. A strange bipping interrupts my dream of rocking gently in a cabin berth with a porthole. Someone in the row in front of me is texting. I wonder who he's talking to at 2.30 in the morning – and what he's talking about. It continues – on and on. He's playing a game on his mobile phone. His wife sleeps serenely next to him. I'm not going to let it worry me. I can handle it. I need to be able to handle it if I'm going to continue travelling. It's the age of technology. There's no way of avoiding gadgets. It does worry me, though, mainly because I can't understand how someone can be so incredibly, unbelievably, thoughtless. *I* wouldn't. I seem to be the only one aggravated, though it's impossible to be sure. There may be others quietly raging all around me. Should I say something, explain that I'm spending the whole day tomorrow on the road and sleep is a priority? He's just far enough away for others to notice and I don't want to create attention. While I've been stewing, he's put his phone away and gone suddenly to sleep. Lucky for him; there's not much chance for me, now. I'll have to go straight through to Arthur River where I'm staying for three nights and catch up on sleep there.

***

By 7am, I'm out onto the Bass Highway.

'Something for breakfast,' I say, vaguely, to the stoney-faced young woman at the bakery at Ulverstone. 'How much is a toasted sandwich?'

'$8.50.'

'$8.50 for a sandwich?' This is not the right time to grumble about prices; she looks like she's had even less sleep than me. She moves from one foot to the other, anxious to get away.

'What about toasted raisin bread?'

'$2.50.' $2.50 sounds okay, though with two slices at $2.50 each, I might as well have had the toasted sandwich. I sit at a table near the window and remind myself of my promise to worry less about money. The food and coffee rejuvenate me and I head along the coast road, stopping periodically to look out over the ocean. It's so beautiful I wonder if I could afford to live here, though if I lived everywhere I liked, I'd have to shift every 12 months.

***

Wynyard is known for its tulips. A large proportion of the tulips exported around Australia are grown here and October is the month they bloom. The town has just had its annual festival, which celebrates the start of the harvest. Tulips sprout in every available spot. I follow the signs to *Table Cape Tulip Farm*. These are not the tulips of my childhood, yellow and all the one shape, matched up with Dutch women in wooden clogs and white hats with wings. Field after field is ablaze with row upon row of colour: deep reds, yellows, pink, purple and orange. It's worth christening my new white runners in the mud from the last week of heavy rain to get closer.

'They're beautiful, aren't they?' says a woman, stooping over a red-striped yellow bloom.

'Beautiful. I didn't even know about this. I was just passing on my way to Arthur River.'

'Oh yes,' she says, 'we come up from Hobart every year.'

'From Hobart?'

'Yes. We're gardeners and every year we come for more bulbs.' She smiles. "It's a bit of an addiction.'

'Lovely addiction to have.' Her husband joins her and they continue along the row. I return to the car, thinking how the experiences you stumble on are often better than those you organise. It's something I love about travelling – waiting to see what's going to happen. It's not always comfortable but almost always interesting – and often, as here, stunningly beautiful.

***

Table Cape is a flat-topped promontory with sheer cliffs dropping to the sea. Named by my old mates, Matthew Flinders and George Bass in 1798, it was settled and developed by the *Van Diemen's Land Company* in the 1820s. Mr. C.B.M. Fenton, a former mariner, kept a light burning in the front window of his house to guide mariners through to the burgeoning port of Wynyard. After several shipping accidents, Table Cape was examined for its suitability for a lighthouse. They took their time; the tower and cottages weren't completed and in service until 1888. Its opening was marred three weeks later when the lighthouse keeper's son died of unknown causes. The entry in the lighthouse log book reads: "Wind south. A strong breeze and misty weather. Employed in the lighthouse and cleaning up around the station. At 5.30pm, Bertie Jackson, son of the head light keeper, departed this life, aged one year and two months."

He was buried near the lighthouse and his grave marked by a fuschia bush. The bush has long since disappeared but locals have recently constructed a memorial to little Bertie.

A plaque is set into a large stone near the edge of the cliff. It reads:

On a nearby property was born FREDERICK MATTHIAS ALEXANDER, 20 Jan 1869 – 10 Oct 1955, Founder of the Alexander Technique, discoverer of fundamental facts about functional human movement, one of the "200 people who made Australia great."

I remember there being great interest in the *Alexander Technique* in the 70s, when many of us were looking for more natural ways of remaining healthy. As a young and promising actor, Frederick's voice would become increasingly hoarse during performances, until he could barely make any noise at all. When told there were no medical causes, he resorted to self-help. After years of observation, he concluded that the proper functioning of his body depended on the correct balance of tension in his entire neuro-muscular system. He developed a technique to encourage and maintain this balance, teaching it from 1894 until his death in 1955. The *Alexander Technique* has been endorsed by scientists and there are now 2500 teachers throughout the world. I'm thrilled to be standing here in the place where this great man was born.

Chapter 16

'I've put you in the same one as last time,' says the young woman at the Arthur River Cabin Park.

I was hoping for that. I love this little cabin with its bright red feature wall and I feel like I've come home. Again, I'm the only one here and I wonder when the tourists come. The park looks different this time. The grey and dark green of winter is now softened by bright sunshine, splashing the trees and bouncing off the roofs of the cabins. There's a gentler, less wild feel to it – not better, just different. I drop my case on the bed. I'm suddenly exhausted but I need to check my booking for tomorrow's *Arthur River Cruise* before giving into sleep.

'I'm not the only one, am I?' I ask the woman behind the booking desk.

'You are for tomorrow, so far. We might get more but I doubt it at this time of day.' I change it to Friday, when around a dozen others are expected. My plan was to spend Friday experiencing the Tarkine, via the *South Arthur Forest Drive*. I'll bring that forward to tomorrow. I slide into bed and sleep for two hours, wake up for a 'Cuppa Soup', toast and a shower and sleep again till 8am.

***

My map directs me to the one-way bridge which crosses the Arthur River near its mouth. It's 30 kilometres to the forest, not a great distance, except that the bitumen has turned to dirt, gravel and potholes. It hadn't entered my head to check the state of the road, ridiculous, considering I'm in Tassie's wilderness, and now I'm wondering whether I should put the car through it. I have no idea what a 1997 *Nissan Pulsar* can handle. It rattles, jolts and complains. It's a good hour back along the highway to the turnoff at Smithton, the route usually recommended to access the South Arthur Forests. Should I risk damage to the car to save time? I turn back to the bridge. My dreams of morning coffee in the forest are fading fast.

'Could I use your toilet by any chance?' I ask the woman in a small fast food shop on the other side of Smithton. 'I can't find a public toilet.'

'No, there isn't one,'

'I'm desperate.'

'We're not supposed to. The Council jacked up on us because everyone was using this place as a public toilet.' Not surprising, seeing they haven't supplied one in the town. 'Well, no-one's around,' she says, noting the pained expression on my face. She motions me to follow her through a little passage leading to a large garage. 'It's a bit rough.'

I'm too grateful to care. Memories flood back of the country dunnies of my childhood with their picket gates for doors and their rough concrete floors. It's devoid of the delicate aroma of ours, though, thanks to sewerage. Back in the shop she hands me some soap and a towel.

'Am I going in the right direction for the Tarkine?'
'You are. Go down this road a few kilometres until you come to a blue and green house and turn right. The bridge at Tayatea is flooded, we've had so much rain, so that's out. But you can go through to Kannunah Bridge.' *The bridge at Tayatea is flooded.* Is that what she said? So the full drive is out. 'The blue and green house on the right ... you can't miss it.'

I've missed it but a sign points me in the right direction and within minutes I'm winding through forest-covered hills. The *South Arthur Forests Drive* is a 130 kilometre loop from Smithton through the South Arthur Forests, which include the Milkshake Hills, Lake Chisholm and Julius River Forest Reserve. It's drizzling as I arrive at Kannunah Bridge. I throw on my old parka, on the floor of the car for just this purpose, and wander down a track, picking my way through mud and moss, to balance on the rocks at the edge of the Arthur River. I breathe deeply. The air is cold and pure. The river surges past, ignoring me and the trees tower above. The hum of the odd mosquito and the bird sounds add to the quietness rather than disturbing it.

'Yoo hoo ... yooo hooo.' I do what everyone does when they can't work out where a sound is coming from. I pretend I didn't hear it. 'Hello-oo.' Two women hang over the railing of the bridge, laughing and waving, as if they've waited their whole lives to meet me. 'Didn't know where it was coming from, did you?' I shake my head, forcing a smile. I'm being invaded by a tourist group. Maybe they won't stay long. The two women plough down the track toward me. They're from rural Victoria and were on the boat the same night as me.

Communing with nature is not on the agenda of these cheerful, empty people. We trudge back up the hill, their chatter ricocheting off me. They don't seem to care where they're heading or even where they've been. I take the chance to question Tony, the bus driver, on the roads and the wear and tear on my car. He's very knowledgeable, having driven these hills for years, and assures me the car will stand up to the gravel road back to Arthur River. It's a great relief – I wasn't looking forward to repeating the trip back through Smithton. I make myself a coffee from my thermos and sit slightly apart from the group, hoping they'll offer me one of their delicious-looking sandwiches. They don't, and as soon as they've finished eating they move out and the silence returns. I don't remember even one of them commenting on the scenery.

Against Tony's advice, I wait for a huge logging truck to pass and continue along the ring road. 'Don't go any further,' he'd said, 'not worth it, nothing there.' 'Nothing there' turns out to be *Sumac Lookout*. Tier upon tier of densely forested mountains spread out before me. In the distance, the dark green of the forest takes on the illusion of a smoky blue, colour co-ordinating with the soft grey of the wintery sky. The Arthur River winds its way through the centre, so far below me it could be just a stream. As usual, photos do no justice but I take one, to remind myself later, when I'm in my cottage, surrounded by concrete and bitumen, of what else is in the world. The road to *Julius River Forest Reserve* is more potholes than anything else and so I add it to my latest list of things to do in the future.

I expected to be directed to forest walks during the 30 kilometres home but I haven't seen one sign. Something I'm coming to terms with is that the expectations you have at the beginning of the trip need constant readjustment. No matter how much research you do, at some stage you have to give up your set ideas and just wait to see what happens. I came here to spend the day walking in the forests. Walking to the river's edge at Kannunnah Bridge has been my only opportunity.

A wide track opens out to my right and I do a quick U-turn. It looks to have been a logging road, no longer in use, from the dead trees that have collapsed across it and grasses that are growing well. The drizzle that dogged me early in the day has gone, allowing the sun to warm me as I wind my way along. Birds dart past and the breeze ruffles the leaves. I sit on a fallen log and watch a lizard scavenging in a hole next to me. He puts his head up, spies me and zips away. A willy-wagtail flits around my feet and I relax, the hard miles of the day easing away.

***

A caravan has turned up during the day and a middle-aged couple sit in the shade of a small annex. It's a lovely feeling to be sharing the park. I open a packet rice concoction, put it in a bowl and place it in the microwave. I don't have a microwave at home and so each time I use one I have to relearn the procedure. Each seems to work differently to the one before and I wonder why they don't make them all the same. Would that be too much to ask or would it make life too easy? Five minutes later it hums into action. I flick on the news.

The Government and, even more so, the Opposition, are turning the grief and suffering of so-called illegal refugees into a political points-scoring exercise. Bizarre, when you thing about it. I'm sitting in an empty cabin park in an almost empty island, in a massive country with a few million people scattered around its edge, being told there's no space for a few hundred extras.

It's dusk and I race down to the beach to catch the sunset. Shafts of rose pink radiate from behind a line of grey-blue clouds, turning their edges a soft violet. It reflects off the water and the waves sparkle and flicker with pink and violet lights. Within minutes the lights fade and the ocean, sand and sky become one.

***

MV George Robinson is a 15.5 metre steel boat, fitted out with Tasmanian timber and brass. It was built in the 1980s, using plans from a 19th century river boat.

'On your go,' says a long-haired man in jeans, brown boots and a bushman's hat. I board with a half a dozen couples. Fold-up chairs provide the seating. I hope we don't hit a wave; it will give a whole new meaning to the term, 'sailing'. The long-haired man is Captain Rob. He introduces his colleague as Mouse, a local woman, open, straight-talking and friendly.

'We'll give it a bit longer,' he says, 'in case anyone's been held up in traffic.' A great gag to open with – traffic is something you don't see a lot of in Arthur River. A safety lesson follows, littered with jokes and a couple rush on at the last minute, wondering why everyone giggles. He starts the engine and we ease away from the dock. I love river cruises, the quietness, the smoothness of the water and the sedate speed. I find myself a spot outside in the bow, wrap my scarf around my neck to protect it from the keen breeze and settle back to listen to the commentary. Arthur River is one of the island's seven major rivers but it's the only one that is completely wild, having never been logged or dammed. No hot fire has passed through the rainforest in almost 650 years. Its remote location has protected its animals and bird life; the only way to explore is on the river.

The cruise takes us 14 kilometres up to the junction of the Arthur and the Frankland rivers. Coastal shrubbery gradually changes to eucalypts and then to rain forest, made up of enormous tree ferns, myrtles, laurels, celery top pines, leatherwoods, sassafras and black wood. Eucalypts grow first to shelter the more delicate trees and ferns. When these are established and the protection is no longer needed, the myrtles release a poison that kills the eucalypts off, allowing more light in. Thus Nature cares for herself.

A pair of White Sea Eagles nests along the bank of the river and waits each day for the boat to arrive. The female is 43 years old and still breeding. She sits high in a tree as we veer toward her and throw a large fish onto the bank. As we quickly reverse, she swoops, seizes the fish and sweeps back to the tree. I made a good decision to watch rather than take a photo as most of the others did. It happened so quickly, I would have missed the photo *and* the experience. The tree where she's sitting is the nursery. The babies are brought here to be taught how to look after themselves. The nest is further along and the father can be seen sitting close to it. Sea eagles are totally wild but have been waiting for titbits from the cruise vessels for 25 years. I relax with a coffee and a biscuit. The myrtles are in bloom and sparkle with rose, gold and orange. A kingfisher darts past and disappears.

Two companies run river cruises and have been given permission to carve out small plots as picnic areas. A large barbecue sits under a canopy at Turk's Landing, next to wooden tables and benches. Mouse prepares lunch while Rob takes us on a nature walk. He was born here, the son of a logger, and knows everything there is to know about the area: the forest, the animals and the disastrous history of the indigenous people. 'They've named it The Tarkine,' he says, 'after the *Tarkiner* aborigines that used to live here. We just call it "the bush".' He delivers the information with a laconic and natural Australian comic timing. In another life he could do stand-up.

The barbecued sausages and hamburgers are tough but I'm too hungry to care. I throw on some salad and a lather of tomato sauce and brave a glass of cask red. We sit quietly eating as the ferns rustle around us and voices murmur. All of the people at my table are middle-aged and inveterate travellers, having explored places as diverse as Antarctica, Singapore and South America. I'm really keen to pick up tips from their experiences but it's like pulling teeth. I wonder that they're not more excited about their travels. I risk boring people to death with mine. When I find a place I love I can't *stop* talking about it. One couple from country Victoria only go home to plan the next trip, but all I can get from them is 'yes' and 'no'. Meeting people who've actually done the trips is the best way, by far, of researching travel so it's a touch frustrating. I clear up after myself and amble away to take photos.

***

It's late afternoon as I drive back to the bridge, park the car and trudge around the sand to where the river joins the sea. Huge waves crash and smash against each other, whipped up by the vicious wind. Seagulls hang in the air, unable to move backwards or forwards. Crossing to the other side of the river, I stand at the lookout. I want to imprint the scene onto my memory so I don't have to leave it behind. Brian Inder feels the same way. An iron plaque is set into a rock and his poem reads:

> *THE EDGE OF THE WORLD*
> *North West Coast Tasmania*
>
> *I cast my pebble onto the shore of eternity*
> *To be washed by the ocean of time,*
> *It has shape, form and substance,*
> *It is me.*
> *One day I will be no more*
> *But my pebble will remain here*
> *On the shore of eternity,*
> *Mute witness for the aeons*
> *That today I came and stood*
> *At the edge of the world.*

Chapter 17

Wynyard is a spotless, thriving town, rattling with Saturday morning traffic. It's here I turn off onto the Murchison Highway on my way to a place called Waratah, a town that looks very unusual in that it has a waterfall in the main street.

'Can I help you,' says a woman, from behind a small desk at the Visitor Centre.

'You may be able to. I'm staying at the Bischoff Hotel in Waratah tonight but it's *Caulfield Cup* Day and I want to make sure I see the race. Do you think they'll have the races on?'

'I'll ring them for you,' she says, 'and find out.' I riffle through a rack of tourist brochures, crossing my fingers the Bischoff has *Channel 7*. You can never be sure what you'll get in the depths of the Tasmanian bush.

'Yes,' says the woman, coming across to me, 'absolutely.'

'Wonderful! I can head straight down then.'

'Here, I'll grab you a map.' She rushes away. Sunshine streams through the large windows. There's a lovely vitality here, an enthusiasm for solving all problems. 'There you go, to stop you getting lost.' I have a map already but she's so eager to help, I take it without comment.

'Lovely place.'

'Yes, it is.' She bustles off.

Paddocks morph into dense forest. I cross the bridge over the Hellyer River and pull into the picnic area at Hellyer Gorge. I park next to an SUV and a small, mud-covered hatchback, a white version of my red one. A couple and their two children sit at a picnic bench, munching on sandwiches and chatting quietly. A young bearded man in jeans and a blue-checked hooded jacket, brown hiking boots splattered with dry mud, sits on a small hill, a backpack beside him, studying something in the grass. The cleared area stops abruptly at what seems a solid wall of trees with a slight opening indicating a track.

'Good morning,' says a middle-aged couple, as they pass me on their way through. The path leads downhill. I immediately start to relax, the tension that always develops when I drive easing away. At the bottom it passes between the river and a stand of large ferns. It's warmer down here, and still, except for a few tiny birds flitting around the undergrowth and a slight breeze rustling the fronds. The river powers past, offsetting the stillness, creating the balance that is Mother Nature.

I'm the only one down here and I wonder why. It's off the beaten track, I guess. You have to make a conscious decision to go west, rather than taking the Midland Highway straight to Hobart and returning via the East Coast, with its beautiful beaches and surfeit of cafes and accommodation. And then, forests are not everyone's cup of tea. There *are* those who find tramping through mud, water decanting down their necks from the surrounding flora, not one of the world's great experiences. I'm only fine with it because the tracks and boardwalks make it easy. Without those the bush would be a far scarier place. The early settlers discovered that. Being lost out here would be terrifying.

***

The Bischoff Hotel was built in 1902 and looks out over Waratah Falls, a wishbone-shaped waterfall that tumbles into the Waratah River. I expected the bar to be filled with men slurping their Saturday afternoon beers and roaring periodically at the television screen as each race is run. It's empty, though, except for two silent men who've obviously spent a lot of time sitting at bars and have seen better days.

'Coral?'

'Yes.'

'I'm Lewis.' He leads me through the rabbit warren of passages that I've come to expect of old pubs, pointing out the kitchen on the way. He's in his early 20s and reminds me of my sons when they were that age.

'Have you worked here long?' I ask.

'It's my parents' hotel.'

'Nothing else around?' I wish I could take that back. It sounds as if there's something wrong with working for your parents.

'Only the mine.'

'I thought it was closed.'

'It reopened last year ... to supply ore for *Renison*.' *Renison Bell* is the large tin mine fifty kilometres to the south.

'You don't fancy working at the mine?' I should be minding my own business but he doesn't seem to mind.

'They bring most of their workers in from Burnie. They're not interested in us.' We turn a corner and continue down another passage. I'm wondering if I'll ever be able to find my way back to the bar when we stop at a door and he inserts the key.

'You're right next to the bathroom so you should be pretty comfortable.' He disappears back into the rabbit warren and I lose my chance of finding out why the mining company prefers workers from Burnie to the locals.

The room is small. A single bed sits in the corner next to a window framed by deep green drapes, held back by plaited cords to let in the light. The carpet matches the curtains. The walls have been covered in ash laminate panelling. There's a tall boy with a small television on top, a coffee table against the wall, a bedside cupboard and lamp, and a wall convection heater. The clash of the dark wood of the furniture with the light wood of the panelling bothers me a little but then I wasn't expecting the Hilton. It's a cosy little nook and has everything I need here for a comfortable night. I drag the racing form from the newspaper I bought at Wynyard and meander back down the stairs.

The bar is at one end of a long room. At the other, lounge chairs and a coffee table surround an enormous flat screen television. A log fire crackles, cheerfully. I order a scotch and *Coke* and set myself up for what's left of the afternoon.

'Another drink?' says Lewis, as he's passing.

'Why not?' The horses are parading for the *Caulfield Cup* when loud voices issue through the front door. Two middle-aged couples enter and line themselves up around the fire. One of the men joins me. The race is won by *Viewed*, last year's *Melbourne Cup* winner, trained by Bart Cummings.

'The Bart Factor', the man says and we nod, knowingly, at each other, as if we have inside info into the Bart Cummings stable and were not the slightest bit surprised. He returns to the group and I edge my way across for a chance of joining in, or at least picking up on their travel stories. It's the thing you can rely on – everyone has travel stories. One woman does most of the talking, her loud, jagged voice cutting the air like a serrated knife. The other is strangely silent and seems to be almost asleep. Maybe she's tired or maybe she didn't want to come in the first place. Her husband sits glowering and I start inventing stories about their relationship and what went wrong with it.

'We've come here because someone told us how friendly it was,' rasps the talker, to Lewis. He pushes drinks across to her. They are all the way from Roma, 500 kilometres north-west of Brisbane. They came from Strahan this morning via Cradle Mountain. I try to get my head around doing the mountainous trip from Strahan, cutting away to Cradle and then back here, and still making it by 3 o'clock, having stopped for lunch on the way. The rough outback voices fill the room, the log fire crackles and the television hums in the background.

I watch the last race and wander outside for a look around. The town of Waratah grew during the heyday of the Mt. Bischoff Tin Mine. James 'Philosopher' Smith was born in July, 1827, near Georgetown. In 1852, he spent time on the Victorian goldfields but returned to Tasmania, where he cleared and farmed a square mile of forest between the Forth and Leven rivers. He was a keen amateur explorer and when on an expedition in December, 1871, he found the first sample of tin ore at Tinstone Creek. Following the creek through to its source he discovered a rich deposit of tin oxide near the summit of Mt. Bischoff.

He was granted two 80-acre mining leases. After his efforts to raise money failed, he sold his farm, organised a bank overdraft and started work. Tin oxide was mined, bagged, taken along the primitive road to Burnie and shipped to England. The returns from this shipment were massive, at which stage money men came from everywhere. *Mt. Bischoff Tin Mining Company* was established in 1873 and Smith was given £1500, 4400 shares and a directorship. It was then that he made one of the less well-considered decisions of his life. He severed his connection with the firm, leaving with a public testimonial of 250 sovereigns, a silver salver and an annual pension of £200. The mine ended up yielding 5,500,000 tonnes of ore and 56,000 tonnes of tin metal. Maybe this philosopher wasn't interested in money. The operation continued until 1929, when a fall in tin prices made it uneconomical. The Commonwealth Government bought it in 1942, as tin was needed for the war effort, and closed it again in 1947.

In the early days of the mine, Waratah was a thriving community, described as "idyllic, nestled amongst a great forest and covered in masses of wildflowers – a bustling place, full of song, music and laughter." The original post office is now a museum and craft centre. You had to be tough to be a postie during the opening up of the west. William Byrne, the first Waratah and West Coast postman, was estimated to have carried the mail 68,000 kilometres during his career, some on horseback but mostly on foot, obstructed by snakes, bogs and swollen rivers. When telegrams brought urgent news, the postmistress delivered them, no matter what the weather or the state of the roads.

That wasn't all she had to put up with. A journalist from The *Tasmanian Mail* visited in 1889 and wrote: "It is quite delicious to visit our post office during wet weather. A constant stream of water flows down the wall onto the sill of the delivery window and bespatters letters and papers and documents in a most impartial manner, and if letters or papers are deposited in the receiving box they float about in a couple of inches of water. The building is an absolute disgrace to the Government ..."

I climb the hill behind the hotel and amble past the primary school. It's impossible to imagine a child being unhappy here. Colours are vibrant, it's spotless and the gardens are filled with tulips and other brilliantly-coloured plants. There is obvious pride in the school even though, at the moment, only 30 children attend. Maybe that accounts for the street being deserted. It's very odd; you'd expect, late on a Saturday afternoon, there would be children careening around on bikes, bouncing basketballs or kicking footballs, but there's not one.

***

It's been a long day and I'm looking forward to a bistro meal. The bar is an entirely different place to when I left. Laughter and chatter explode through the open door. The clink of glasses joins with the clatter of crockery and cooking smells emanate from somewhere in the back. A woman materialises beside me.

'Are you the lady that's staying on her own?' she asks.

'Yes.'

'My husband and I are staying tonight, as well. Would you like to join us?'

'Thanks,' I say, surprised. 'That would be lovely.'

'We're over there. Just come across when you're ready.'

I stand at the bar for an interminable amount of time, waiting to order my meal. The woman taking the orders keeps looking through me, as if I'm invisible. Lewis hangs in the background, lost. I'm assuming the woman is his mother. She could do with his help – she's looking extremely harassed. There comes a time to be assertive. 'Excuse me.' The woman sees me for the first time. 'I'll have the fish and chips.' She adds my order to her list. An arm waves at me from a table at the other end of the room and I work my way through the crowd and across to it.

'I'm Val,' she says. 'We'll sit here. David's talking fishing.' A man on the next table smiles at us and turns back to his companions. I pick their ages to be around 70.

'Where are you from?' I ask.

'Victor Harbor in South Australia. We're beef farmers.'

'I drove through there once.' I had sold my house and had a month to fill in before shifting into the new one. I took the Great Ocean Road, stopping at Aireys Inlet for a visit with my brother and his family. The Princes Highway took me to Adelaide and I stopped at Victor Harbour on the way through. I came back down through central Victoria. At the time I hadn't given in to pressure to buy a mobile phone, and so, with no phone number and no address, I floated free. 'Anything could have happened to you,' my daughters said to me, 'and we wouldn't have known.' I hadn't thought of that. But it didn't, and it was marvellous being separated from the burden of material possessions for just a little while. Everyone should have the experience – regularly. 'Lovely place, Victor Harbor.'

'I have another farm further to the north that I run myself,' says Val.

'You must be energetic.'

'Workaholic, probably. I didn't want to leave the farms but the kids talked us into it. They offered to keep an eye on things while we're away.' I can never understand people having to be talked into travelling. Victor Harbour to Tasmania is hardly adventurous, but then, I guess if you're happy where you are, you wouldn't want to leave. 'They're trying to talk us into going to England next year. Our son lives there.'

'England. Fabulous.' She looks unsure, as if home is the only safe place.

'Fish and chips?' says Lewis, placing a large plate of food in front of me.

'Could I have it down a bit,' I say, pointing to the television behind us, still on from this afternoon.

'Oh, sure.' He adjusts the volume to a bearable level, though why televisions have to be on in a packed bistro, I don't know. Val is happy to talk and I'm happy to listen. The friendly, cheerful ambience of the place envelops me. The fish is delicious and I polish off every skerrick. Suddenly, I'm exhausted.

'It's been a huge day,' I say. 'I think I'll go up.'

'Okay.'

'Where are you off to tomorrow?'

'Strahan for two nights.' She stands and starts dragging her chair across to the next table. 'Then Hobart.'

'The other direction for me.'

'Nice to have met you.' Her husband makes space for her and she turns away. It was very generous of her to think of me. It's the sort of thing you come across when you're travelling. In fact, sometimes I think it's almost a necessity to go out of your comfort zone to find out how thoughtful people can be.

The TV remote is 'on the blink' but just as well. Better that I sleep. Tomorrow I'm working my way via *Gunns Plains Caves* to Leven Canyon. The B15 will then take me through Sheffield and on to Deloraine, where I will stop for three nights. I'm dozing as my mates from Roma pound along the passage and into the kitchen. Maybe they're making coffee – they've been drinking non-stop since mid-afternoon. Doors open and thump shut. Laughter filters up from the street as the bistro empties. Engines rev in the cold air and fade into the night, leaving only the rustling of the river. I snuggle further into my electric blanket, thinking how lucky I am to be cocooned in a warm and friendly hotel, rather than a generic motel room, in a strange and interesting town with a waterfall in the main street. A night bird chirps and I fall asleep.

***

There are those who can drink for hours and then get up the next day as if nothing has happened. This is my friends from Roma. Maybe they're used to it – they're not the healthiest-looking people I've ever seen. They launch themselves into the kitchen and have eaten and are out the door while I'm still looking for the cereal. Val and David nod as they pass the kitchen on their way out. Both cars are gone before my bread is out of the toaster. I make a mental note to become more organised. If I could get out that quickly, I would have a lot more time in the day.

A heavy mist adds to the Sunday morning silence as I cross the road opposite the hotel to the small park that overlooks the river and the waterfall. Given more time I would have taken the walk up to the mine. It's a frustrating part of planning a trip. You don't really know what you want to see until you get there, and then you discover you haven't allowed time for it. On the way out I stop at the *Kenworthy Stamper Mill*. Dudley R. Kenworthy was one of the characters of the district. Born in 1911, he worked in the engineering shop at the mine through the 1940s. After the closure, he and seven others took on their own small lease, cutting down ore and crushing it at the old Waratah battery.

When the partnership broke up, Dudley moved to Burnie to make an 'honest' living. After retiring, he returned to the mountain and built his own single head Stamper Mill, housing it in an old rusted tin shed. A photo shows the area around the shed covered in snow. It must have been bitterly cold in winter. As I was once told by a friend who mined opals at White Cliffs, 'it gets in your blood'. The mill has been brought into the town by locals and restored to full working capacity.

Chapter 18

The mist is turning to light rain as I return to the car. The mountains loom in the distance, drawing the river along into their dark, primeval forests. It must have been a bleak place at times in the early days of the mine, cold, foggy and wet. Still, a large part of the population came from mining towns in the British Isles so I guess cold, foggy and wet would be the norm. I know, though, that with the sun out, it will be one of the prettiest places around.

A few kilometres out of town the road leads past a swathe of land that has been logged and I stop to take a photo. It's a horrifying scene, as if some huge monster has moved in and demolished everything in sight before moving on, which is pretty much what has happened. I take the turnoff that leads across to Gunns Plains and down to Leven Canyon. The forest is behind me for the moment. With every turn in the road I'm greeted with another gentle, glorious vista. The misty rain of this morning has gone and sunshine caresses everything. Cows dream on the sides of grassy hills and two eagles float above the earth.

***

A beautiful forest track leads me to a large cantilevered platform, suspended and directed out over the canyon. Halfway out my fear of heights symptoms dig in. I close my eyes and hold tightly to the railing, breathing deeply. Intellectually, I know I'm safe but it doesn't help. And it doesn't matter. Halfway is good, looking out across the ever-present layers of forest-covered mountains, with a glimpse, if I lean forward just slightly, of the Leven River.

The Leven Valley was explored by timber cutters and settlers in the 1850s, but had been discovered by the indigenous *North Tribe* centuries before, and mapped through shared stories. They passed through here as part of their seasonal migration, hunting on inland plains kept clear by regular fires, and moving to the coast in winter to avoid the extreme cold and heavy snow. They must have been quite powerful in terms of trade, as most of the highly-prized ochre, used to paint the hair and body, originated in their territory.

Steps have been installed in a track down to the floor of the canyon – 697 of them. 697? I'll *do* it! Periodic seating has been added to curtail the incidence of heart failure. Step numbers are carved into the seats to tell you where you've been and how far you've got to go. It was constructed by Stephen McTurk, Central Coast track specialist. Stephen and his crew carried bags of cement equivalent to the weight of three cars, along with 132 posts and 550 litres of water for mixing the cement. It took almost a year on freezing days of -2°C through to summer heat of more than 30°C.

The river at the bottom of the gorge is a stream, at best, bordered, as usual, by enormous ferns. A little bridge leads across to the other side. Birds dart through the trees, butterflies flit around the rustling undergrowth and the water ripples by me. I could happily remain here for hours but I've just realised walking down means walking up again. Luckily, there's an alternative route back. Climbing 697 steps *would* kill me. I wonder how often they look for bodies. The pathway is almost perpendicular. I stop often to get my breath back and allow my heart to slow. Spider webs brush my face. Mosquitoes attack. The forest suddenly opens out to the car park.

Lunch in a bush spot is a delight. Some people prefer their holidays to be spent in the hype of say, Vegas or Rio, or even the Gold Coast. I'm completely content with a coffee from my thermos and a salmon and avocado sandwich from my esky, though I wouldn't knock back Vegas or Rio if it was offered. It's 1.30pm and I pack up and retrace the 12 kilometres of winding road to the B15. On the way to Deloraine are villages with names like Lower Crackpot, Promised Land and Nowhere Else. I'm keen to check them out but when I get close, find they're not *on* the main road, as the map shows, but several kilometres off. You'd need six months if you wanted to explore every country lane, or a year, or maybe you'd need to live here.

***

Sheffield is known for the murals on the side of its public buildings, showing the history of the area. It's a nice little town and I shout myself some lavender oil and soap from a pretty gift shop. Coffee and to-die-for cream cake follow. I remind myself about my food intake. It would be quite easy to end up like a lot of middle-aged tourists I'm seeing around – extremely large, red, and panting when they move.

***

My motel room at the Mountain View Country Inn in Deloraine is far from new but has everything I could possibly need. A picture window looks over green paddocks to the dolomite crags of the Great Western Tiers. I hang up my shirts and jeans and arrange my toiletries in the bathroom. It's a great relief to have a comfortable place as my base for the two days and three nights that I'll be in the area. I wake to bright sunshine and blue sky. Today, I'm covering territory I tried to cover three months ago. I'm passing through the villages of Westbury and Longford to *Clarendon Estate*.

Chapter 19

The only sounds, as I sit at a picnic table in the grounds of *Clarendon*, with my coffee and a sandwich, come from the chortling of magpies and a lawn being mown somewhere in the distance. I gaze across at the three storeys of white Georgian mansion, rising, regally, from the gardens surrounding them. Two flights of steps lead to a large portico, framed, theatrically, by four imposing Grecian columns. James Cox wanted to make a statement.

James was born in 1790, the second son of Captain William Cox of Devizes, Wiltshire. His parents left him to be educated at *King Edward's Grammar School*, in the shadow of *Salisbury Cathedral*, while they set up a property on the Hawkesbury River in New South Wales. He joined them in 1806 to help run their, by then, two estates of *Clarendon* and *Fernhill*, during his father's three year absence in England.

He married Mary Connell in June, 1812, at the age of 22. I'm not sure how happy James's parents would have been with his choice of bride. She was the daughter of John and Catherine Connell, who were convicted of receiving stolen goods in the form of a pair of shoes, both, strangely, the same foot. The young man who stole them, a ten-year-old named William Hill, was confined for seven days and ordered to pay one shilling. John Connell was let off and Catherine was transported for 14 years. Work *that* one out.

In 1814, James was granted 700 acres at Morven, now Evandale, successfully petitioning for a further 6000. It was considered unsafe at the time to live there, due to the constant threat of bushrangers and the ongoing skirmishes with the local indigenous tribes. He settled his wife and three children in Launceston and became a wholesale merchant, with a government contract to supply meat to the settlements at Launceston and Georgetown. Moving to *Clarendon* in the mid 1820s, he began designing his mansion. The house was eventually finished in 1838.

With the help of a particularly virile Spanish ram named 'Newton', his merino flock grew. He also imported a fine Hereford bull, with whose stock he gained many prizes. He imported fallow deer, established a hunt and emulated the lifestyle of an English country gentleman. He sired eight children with Mary, who died after delivering the last child in 1828. Within a year he married Eliza Eddington, daughter of Lieutenant-Governor David Collins, a serious step up from his last choice. Eliza gave birth to 11 children, eight of whom survived their childhood. James and 'Newton', it seems, had a lot in common.

Clarendon is the perfect example of the English upper-class, 'upstairs downstairs', family home. Servants' quarters and the kitchen were on the lower floor, while the family lived above. Farm workers were housed on the estate, along with convicts and their guards. It must have been a very interesting life, cocooned here, everyone interacting with and reliant on everyone else. I spend two hours wandering the property: the coach house and large stables, the round shepherd's cottage, its roof rising to a point at the centre, (I envy the shepherd; I've always wanted to live in a round house), the barns and woolshed and the stone convict quarters and guard house. There's a tiny, Gothic-style cottage, straight out of a story book, its roof peaked and its gorgeous little windows latticed. It has to have at least housed the gardener but no, it was a toilet block.

It's a very expensive proposition maintaining a *National Trust* property as large as *Clarendon* and in the 1960s it was almost discarded. However, it received a reprieve from the Federal Government and has just been allotted $900,000 for desperately needed repairs. I hope it continues. It's an important part of our colonial history, and anyway, it's too lovely to lose.

***

I passed through Evandale too quickly on my last trip so this time I'm stopping to have a good look around. A side street, off the main road, curves past beautifully kept heritage cottages to a pretty park. A crop of gravestones sprouts from the grass. An old lady stands opposite, at the gateway of a white, weatherboard house, waving to a man pulling away in a car. She waits for me to cross the road and I know I'm cornered.

'That's my nephew,' she says.

'Is it?' She watches the car till it turns the corner at the end of the street.

'He helps me out.'

'Right.'

'Since my husband died.'

'Ooh ... I'm sorry.' I consider moving on but something holds me back. 'Was he sick?'

'No, he wasn't sick. He went into the hospital in Launceston.' Her hand trembles as she runs it over her white hair. 'It was just an overnight stay ... nothing, really.'

'What happened?'

'I went in the next day to see him and he was in Intensive Care.'

'Intensive Care? Why?'

'He had pneumonia. They tried to make me sign a form to let him die.'

'*What?*' She leans against the gate post as if the shock has just been delivered.

'I said no but they kept asking ... they were *so* mean.'

'Did they tell you what happened?'

'No, they wouldn't tell me. Just that I had to sign the form.' She looks directly at me for the first time. 'How could I? We were married for 53 years. How could I let him die?' I can hardly believe what she's telling me but she's obviously too close to the experience to be able to do anything other than relate it as it happened. 'My nephew came in with me to help but they wouldn't tell him either. They were *so mean*.' They'd have told me. I'd have rampaged around the place until they did.

'He used to do everything.' She turns and waves her arm at the front yard. 'I suppose I could try working the lawn mower, but ...' We gaze, silently, as the bright sun flickers through the branches of a white magnolia tree in the centre of the lawn, creating shadowy patterns on the grass beneath it. 'He wanted to be buried opposite the house,' she says, turning back to look across at the little cemetery.

I feel desperately sorry for her. After 53 years of marriage her husband is suddenly gone. Not being told why only makes it worse. On top of that, she's groping with legal matters. As was the fashion of the times, everything was in her husband's name. It cost her $1900 just to get the title of the house transferred to her. I wish her well. As I leave, she crosses the road to her husband's grave. I watch her lean over a little vase and make adjustments to the flowers.

***

I had always thought that *Franklin House*, the *National Trust* property in Franklin Village, eight kilometres south of Launceston, was something to do with Sir John Franklin, Governor of Tasmania, but no. It was built by Britton Jones, ex-convict and successful inn-keeper, as a rental property. Jones leased it to William Keeler Hawkes and his wife, Martha, in 1842. They added a classroom and opened *The Classical and Commercial School*. Many of the sons of the local gentry were educated here, including those of James Cox of *Clarendon*. It would have been a tough life for the boys. They were boarders, only going home during two holidays: Christmas and mid-year. School was six days a week and on Sundays they went to church – twice. William Keeler was a strict disciplinarian, with a liking for corporal punishment. I drift around the first floor bedrooms and the refurbished schoolroom.

Little voices echo, endlessly repeating times-tables. I fancy I hear the swish of a cane as it descends on a young bottom or a naked, outstretched hand.

Kitchen gardens were essential in country estates. They had to provide vegetables and fruit for the whole family and the servants and, in the case of *Franklin House*, the students. A lot of research went into re-establishing this garden, using the original Victorian plans. All of the plants grown are of the era of the house and are used in the tea room in soups, frittata and as garnishes. Any extras are sold for funds to buy new seeds. Some have names such as China Rose Radish, Violet Sicilian Cauliflower and Drunken Woman Lettuce. I'd like to see *that* one. Magnificent oak trees shade the flower gardens and the gazebo, and tulips bloom everywhere. It's a surprisingly small property, compared with *Clarendon* and estates such as *Ripponlea* and *Como House* in Melbourne. The stables are so close to the house you could just about lie in bed and hear the horses snoring.

Chapter 20

It's been raining over night and the road works outside of Deloraine pack the wheels and the car itself with yellow mud. A sign directs me along five kilometres of narrow, slippery, winding, mountainous road to Liffey Falls. Picnic tables sit in a cleared area in the centre of Liffey Forest. It's cool but not cold enough for a coat as I follow the walking track into the trees. The river running alongside is surprisingly shallow, compared with the wild ones I've become used to and ripples over rock that's been shaped into mosaic patterns over aeons. An avenue of huge tree ferns leads me gently downwards. The sun filters through the trees as the pathway becomes a boardwalk and voices drift up to me.

A group of half a dozen men and women stand at a lookout, nattering quietly. They move aside to make space for me. The waterfall emerges from a backdrop of Myrtle, Sassafras and Leatherwood trees, spilling over three tiers of rock and gushing past me to disappear back into the forest. This *is* the prettiest place I've ever been. The group leaves me to myself and I sit on a bench facing out toward the endless, thickly forested, mountains. A feeling of well-being settles on me as I gaze through the tree tops, releasing the anxiety of navigating my way around the narrow, muddy road to get here.

***

On my first trip I fell in love with the caves at Mole Creek and promised myself a return visit. The sun is beating down now that I've left the forest and the car is chugging ominously. The *Chudleigh Honey Farm*, where I planned to have lunch, is closed. The tourist brochure *and* the website say they're open during the week. So much for tourist brochures and websites. Lunch at the convenience store is fatty bacon and fried egg on white, cardboard-tasting bread, and a milkshake. The car shudders as I turn onto the dirt road leading to the caves and I lose my nerve. I can't risk breaking down on a dirt track in the bush so I'll have to add that to my 'things for the future' list. The car makes it to the top of the motel driveway before giving in.

'Seems to be alright,' says the extremely corpulent man from the *RACT*. He opens the bonnet and jiggles a few bits. 'Can't see anything.' Getting back into the driver's seat he revs the engine again – hard. Maybe that's it. Maybe I'm just not putting enough energy into it.

'Oh well, never mind,' I say, which is what I always say to tradesmen when they find nothing wrong with an appliance that, until they arrived, refused to work. 'I'll try it myself before you go, just to make sure.'

'No worries.' I start the engine three times, sign the form and he leaves.

***

There's a lot of history attached to Latrobe. It was first settled by Europeans in 1826, when my old mate, Edward Curr of *Highfield Estate* at Stanley, through his management of the *Van Diemen's Land Company*, established *North Down*, the first major property in the district. Situated on the Mersey River, Latrobe developed because it was the first convenient crossing point. Ferries came up the river to the town and it became a thriving port. It was named after Charles Latrobe, who, at the time, was acting Lieutenant-Governor of Van Diemen's Land and subsequently, Lieutenant-Governor of Victoria. For most of the 19th century, it was the most important town on the north coast. Inevitably, it was outstripped by Devonport and by the early 1900s, the town had slipped into decline. It revived in the 1970s with the establishment of a number of wood fibre and paper mills and is now popular as a retirement location and as suburban overspill from Devonport.

Last time I was here, one of the old pubs in the main street was offering accommodation but when I asked for a room, it was painfully obvious that I was putting the proprietor out and seriously getting in his way. At that stage it was too dark to start looking around for something else that I could afford and so I put up with the unpleasant atmosphere and the cigarette stench that permeated every inch of the bedroom. This time I'm aiming for something better, an en suite cabin, at least.

'There's the caravan park,' says the woman at the tourist and information centre, 'but I think they only have two cabins.'

'Only two?'

'They're renovating.' She gives me the names of a couple of holiday parks in East Devonport.

The road leading out of town winds through gentle forest to where the river opens out to its full width. It's very grand and I park and sit looking across to the city of Devonport. The car coughs as I start it and I'm wondering if it's going to make it back to Melbourne. I have a nightmarish picture of it breaking down on the ship's ramp and blocking all the traffic coming off.

'I know a bloke, I can give you 'is name,' says the woman at the caravan park near the ferry terminal. I've probably made a wrong choice. It's a rough-looking place and the woman is rougher. Still, she's friendly and knows someone who fixes cars. 'He's been 'ere today doin' mine,' she says, 'he's good and sometimes he can come straight away.'

'Thanks. I'll see how it goes.' It might be worth a try but then I've only got one day to go and a strange mechanic can be risky.

The cabin is old, with a one element stove barely working, no central light and an ancient couch that reeks so badly of cigarettes, I think I'd be ill if I sat on it. The tiny television is a *Telefunken*. I haven't seen one of those for decades. They were made to last in those days. There's an argument going on in the caravan opposite me – loud voices. I hope that's as far as it goes.

'Is there a supermarket around?' I ask, sticking my head through the door of the office.

'Turn right out of the gates, luv, and keep goin'.'

'Walking distance?'

'Yep.'

The caravan park joins the beach which overlooks Bass Strait and the ferry terminal is a short walk along the sand. It's a working-class area, apart from a few old Victorian-style homes dotted about, though mansions are being built on the hills overlooking the ocean. It's a beautiful spot and I'm surprised it's taken this long to be discovered.

I'd forgotten about *Rice'a'Riso*. I thought it had been discontinued but there it was on the shelf. Thoughts of weekend lunches made easy flood my mind and guilt invades me with the first bite. I can't believe I fed this to my children. That was when manufacturers were introducing us to instant food and we couldn't believe our luck. We were definitely not discerning in those days and, considering how many people still live on takeaway, nothing's changed.

***

It's dusk, clear and warm, as I stand on the sand looking out across the water. A horn blasts and I realise the *Spirit* is leaving for the crossing. I dash down in time to join others as her massive form crawls along the river.

Chapter 21

I'm spending my last morning back in Latrobe and this time I'm determined to have a good look around. What I find amazes me. Street after street of stunning heritage homes, each one different to the next. The gardens are just as beautiful. One even has its own stream running through. I want one. Looking through beautiful parkland toward the river is *Sherwood Hall*, one of the most unique colonial homes in Australia. Built by Thomas and Dolly Dalrymple Johnson in 1850, it was constructed using mortise and tenon joints instead of nails. Its roof is shingled and the ceilings are notched to fit the walls.

I'm greeted by an enthusiastic young woman, who insists I begin my tour by putting in ear buds and listening to a five minute blurb on the history of the house and the remarkable people that built it. Thomas Johnson was transported for burglary in 1824. Dolly was born around 1810 on the Furneaux Islands, the daughter of Worrete-moete-yenner and sealer, George Briggs. As the first half-caste born in the colony, she was taken from her mother around the age of two and adopted by Dr. Jacob Mountgarret and his wife, Bridget, of Port

Dalrymple. Baptized Dalrymple, she was taught reading, writing and domestic skills. I try to envisage having my toddler ripped away from me, never to see her again, but it's beyond me. What would that do to a mother? What would it do to the child?

Dolly left the Mountgarrets in 1828 to live with Thomas in a log and bark dwelling at Dairy Plains, where he worked as a stockman. In 1831, while Thomas was away working, Dolly spent six hours protecting her young children from attack by a group of aborigines. For her bravery she was granted 20 acres of land. Thomas received a pardon and they married two months later. They chose Perth to settle but were treated badly by the locals, who disapproved of an Aborigine and an ex-convict being allowed to own land. Thomas was again found guilty of burglary in the form of receiving stolen wheat and was sentenced to seven years. By this time, Dolly was expecting her fifth child and without Thomas's income, life was tough. She wrote to Governor Arthur, requesting that Thomas be retained as her servant but was denied. Governor Arthur was not known for his benevolent nature.

Thomas returned home in 1841 and, in 1845, they settled in Latrobe. Thomas, by this stage, must have got his act together because from then on they prospered, developing a successful business, turning timber into palings for export to the mainland. In 1850, they built *Sherwood Hall*. They bought two hotels and built a community centre, used for church services, meetings and, during the week, as a school. Coal was discovered on their property and the *Alfred Colliery* opened in 1855. They built the *Native Youth Hostel* and constructed roads and bridges, all while bringing up 13 children. *Sherwood Hall* was brought, piece by piece, to Bell's Parade and restored. It was opened on 26th November 1995, the 150th anniversary of Thomas and Dolly's settlement in the area. It's a marvellous story. Someone should make a movie.

***

When I visited the home of former Prime Minister Joseph Lyons and his wife, Dame Enid, three months ago, the house was closed for winter. This time I've organised well. I've checked my brochure several times and I'm well inside the opening hours. *Home Hill* was built in Devonport in 1916. Joseph was Premier of Tasmania from 1923 to 1928. He became Prime Minister in 1932 and died in office in April, 1939. When Enid Lyons became Prime Ministerial wife, she was aged 33 and the mother of 11 children. She used her position to promote women's and family issues. It's said her speeches were so good that Prime Minister Robert Menzies, known for his speeches, avoided sharing the platform with her. She was knighted in recognition of her work in 1937, on an official visit to England for the coronation of *King George VI*.

Four years after her husband's death she was elected the first female member of the Cabinet. After retiring in 1951, she became a newspaper columnist and a commissioner of the *Australian Broadcasting Corporation*. She died in 1981. She was one of the most outstanding women in Australia's history, even more so in that she spent most of her life in chronic pain. She had suffered a fractured pelvis during the birth of her first child, which wasn't discovered till later in life, after a further 11 children. As the old cliché goes, 'they don't make 'em like that anymore'.

The car chugs up the hill in the early afternoon sunshine. The driveway to the car park is blocked off. Workmen moving soil from one spot to another watch, half-interestedly, as I stroll up to the door. The house is closed, though there's nothing to say it is; there's just no-one here. It's infuriating when they put their opening times in brochures and on the web *and* on the front door of the house, and then don't bother turning up. I seethe as I sit on a garden bench under the wisteria. It's another to add to my list of 'next times', though I don't know whether I'd bother again. I might just 'spit the dummy' and not come back. Probably will, though. It's gorgeous – I'm desperate to look inside.

***

It's still daylight as the ship glides along the river. I sit on a large metal box attached to the deck and watch Tasmania retreat. An elegant, middle-aged woman and her husband sit beside me. She tells me about an enormous tree they discovered in the Franklin River region, moss descending from the trunk onto its massive roots and into the ground, like a huge velvety ball gown.

'I call her the Duchess,' she says. 'That's what she seemed to me. The Duchess of the Forest. And would you believe, there was not one other person around.' She turns to her husband.

'No-one,' he says. I understand what they're telling me. You can discover something so beautiful, so perfect, and no-one else seems interested enough to even look. Lights blink on from the shoreline as we move out into the waves of Bass Strait.

'Bye, Tassie,' she says. 'Thanks.' The breeze stiffens and becomes wind and passengers start moving inside. The smell of food from the buffet entices as the door opens and closes.

'You hungry?' he says. She nods and they take each others' hands and drift away.

'I've ridden my bike around the coastline three times,' says a man from the centre of a group of drinkers further along the deck. 'Twenty years I've been coming here.'

I can see the attraction. It's partly that it's so easy. Drive onto a ship and drive off the next morning and you're on your way, in the vehicle you understand and are comfortable with. There's more to it, though. The more places I see, the more I want to see – those still waiting to be discovered: the Huon Valley and Hastings Caves, the tourist icon of Cradle Mountain and the Bay of Fires and Mt. William National Park, and those I love and long to return to: the caves at Mole Creek, Arthur River, breathtaking Great Oyster Bay and the wild, battered coastline of the Tasman Peninsula. I could be coming back here forever; it could become addictive. Obviously, for this man, it has. And why not? Riding your motor bike through rainforest sounds like a pretty healthy addiction to me. The ship rocks and I watch the lights on the shore fade into pinpoints and disappear.

'Bye, Tassie ... Thanks.'

The Edge of the World – Next Stop Cape Horn

March 2012

Chapter 22

It's a beautiful Melbourne autumn day. The sun flashes off the skyscrapers and the whole of Port Phillip Bay sparkles and glitters. It seems like yesterday that I sat here on the deck of The *Spirit*, a glass of red wine in my hand, waiting for the throbbing of the engines, but it's actually two and a half years. I feel like an old 'pro' as first-timers pass me, families with excited children straining over the railing, agog at the drop beneath them. A tense man paces backwards and forwards in front of me, conducting some sort of business on his mobile phone. Two smokers huddle in a corner with the haunted look smokers have these days, demonised as they are.

I'm a first-timer myself in a way. I've taken the advice of the woman at The *Stranded Whale* cafe in Stanley who, after I complained about the discomfort of the 'luxury' recliners, said, 'Do what I do. Book a cabin and hope no-one else turns up. It's worked for me.' It hasn't worked; I've already met my cabin mate and I'm a little anxious about the whole thing. I have no idea of the politics of sharing such a small place with a stranger. She, on the other hand, was far too distracted to care about politics.

'Oh, my God!' she said, bursting through the door, her eyes glassy with adrenalin. 'I didn't think I was going to make it.'

'Why is that?'

'I missed the turn-off and ended up in the city.'

'Oh, my God!' I consider the nightmarish scenario of being lost in Melbourne's late afternoon traffic. 'I never drive in the city,' which is not a useful thing to say but it seemed to have a calming effect on her.

'But it's alright,' she said, 'I found my way back. She dropped her bag onto the opposite bed. 'I've been driving since this morning.'

'You're not from Melbourne, then?'

'No, I'm from north of Sydney but I stayed with friends in Lakes Entrance overnight.'

'Lakes Entrance? Long drive.'

'I'd love a shower,' she said, searching the cell for some sign of an en suite. I pointed to the door at the end of my bed. 'Great.' She started rummaging through her bag and I left her to it.

I have plans in place for my fourth trip to Tassie but I know they can change at any time. Tassie has a way of doing that to you. I'm retracing my steps through Waratah to Queenstown and along the Lyell Highway. The Franklin River awaits me, as does gorgeous Nelson Falls and, for the first time, the giant trees of the Styx Valley. A couple of days on foot in Hobart will give me a break from the car. I'm hoping for some sunshine or, at least, temperatures above the 8° of my first visit. From there, the east coast will take me through St. Helens to the Blue Tiers of the north-east and across for another look at the Mole Creek Caves.

It's almost dark as the ship churns its way toward Port Phillip Heads. I say a silent goodbye to my children, take a last look at the city and move inside to the warmth and the aromas of the buffet. Around nine o'clock, I quietly open the door to the cabin. To my surprise, the woman is already asleep. I guess she's exhausted from her less than relaxing day. I pop in the ear plugs I thought to bring – there's a hint of snoring already – and allow the ship to rock me to sleep.

'I'm a writer,' she says, the next morning, as we're dragging ourselves into some semblance of order.

'Me, too,' I say, surprised, though I shouldn't be. Many middle-aged people take up writing, thrilled that they at last have time to do something entirely for themselves. 'I'm still a novice, though. Have you been writing long?'

'I've been putting words together all of my life.' She is booked into a cabin for five weeks in the little town of Snug, partly to catch up with her son, who is at university in Hobart and partly to work on a biography of an extremely interesting-sounding aunt. The time away is also a respite from a demanding husband and a very demanding and cantankerous, 97-year-old mother-in-law.

'I do everything for her,' she says. 'If she needs to go to hospital, needs help of any sort, I do it. None of her kids do a thing for her.'

'Typical.'

'It's my house. They both came to live with me.' She pauses but I know there's something else. I smile to encourage her. 'I shouldn't whinge but they treat me like a servant. She had friends round one time to look at the garden. When they asked who I was, she told them I was the housekeeper. She had a glint in her eye when she said it. She knew what she was doing.'

'Bit of an old 'bugger', I think.'

'The trouble is everyone tells me how wonderful she is.'

'They would. Funny how people assume someone's wonderful just because they're old.'

'And I can't say anything.'

'Of course not. You'd look bad. They'd judge you.'

'She's really healthy. I think ... you know ... she'll outlive me.'

'Oh, dear.' I wish her well with her writing and her domestic problems. I wonder what she'll decide. It's time she moved them on, as far as I'm concerned. No-one should be treated like a servant, especially in their own home.

***

I wind through green paddocks, dotted with freshly-milked cows, on my way to Leven Canyon. The air is cool and fresh, the sun is shining and the sky is a pale blue. Snow scatters the peaks of the Black Buff mountain range in the distance. It's beautiful, it's peaceful, it's Tassie. I'm surprised, as I enter the beautifully maintained car park and picnic area. You can get your National Parks mixed up after a while; my mind had this one attached to Hellyer Gorge. My breath turns to fog as I leave the car. A little girl, running around on the grass on her own, stops to stare at me. I wave to her and she breaks into a smile and waves back. Unusual – children are very careful who they wave at these days. It's a 20 minute walk to the platform out over the canyon. Profuse ferns swish lightly in the breeze, leading the eye upwards to the grey of eucalypt trunks against a background of almost white sky. It's like being inside a painting.

It's funny how you remember things. The last time I was here, the platform out over the canyon seemed much longer, prompting all my usual fear of heights symptoms. Now I realise it's only half that length. I lean against the railing, still not able to reach the end, and look out over the ranges of the Leven Canyon Reserve. Voices tinkle up from the track, and a child's laughter. The little girl skips past me, her young mother following behind. They continue, without thought, to the end of the platform and stare down at the Leven River far below. The woman turns and smiles at me.

'It's a beautiful place, isn't it?'

'Yes,' she says. 'We arrived yesterday just for a look and couldn't leave.'

'You stayed here last night?'

'Yes. You're not supposed to but others were, so we did, too.'

'In your car?'

'No, we've got a van.'

'You're not from Tassie, then?'

'We live in Adelaide. We left four months ago.'

'You've been touring around Tassie for four months?'

'Yes.'

'Just the two of you?'

'Yes.'

'How wonderful!' It's what I would do if I gave myself the chance – wander for months at a time. One day I will.

'We'll have to go soon, though. It's getting too cold. Last night we couldn't use the tent.'

'You've been pitching a tent?'

'Most nights.' She runs her hand lightly over her daughter's hair. The child darts away back to the track and investigates a hole in a log. 'It's lucky we were in the van. Some 'hoons' turned up and rampaged around for hours. They left a terrible mess.'

'Mummy, look,' calls the child, pointing to the log. The mother nods.

'Your little girl isn't at school, yet?' I ask. She would be well into school age.

'She's home-schooled.' A shadow alters her bright, open face. 'You hear different things about school?' It's a question, a surprising one. What does she mean? Hasn't she been to school? She looks Asian; maybe she didn't go to school here and so doesn't know what to think about it. 'Kids she knows tell her that school is awful,' she says. It's at this stage I realise the child is standing next to us, taking in every word. It's very sad to leave her with this idea. School deals with a lot more than the academic. How will she learn to interact socially if she remains tied to her mother?

Still, who's to say? Given the choice between touring Australia and spending each day chained to a strict school routine, I know which one I'd choose. She's a very confident little girl – she may just cope with whatever is dished up. It's fascinating how beliefs govern our behaviour. This young woman is completely comfortable camping on her own in the wilderness, something most travellers, even with a partner, would think twice about, and yet she's too afraid to let her child go to school. She wanders away to look out over the canyon. The child stays.

'Are you frightened?' she asks.

'A little bit,' I answer, surprised.

'Why?'

'Well, it's a bit high up here.' She looks through the railings to the huge rocks leading down the cliff and then back at me, as if I'm one of the weirder people she's run into.

'I'm not frightened,' she says.

'You're not?'

'No.' To demonstrate, she skips to the end of the platform and back again.

'You're brave.' The mother joins us. Her face is again open and relaxed.

'That's the path down to the valley, isn't it?' she asks, pointing to the steps.

'Yes. There are 697 steps down but a path takes you back to the car park. You don't have to climb back up them.'

'Okay.' She takes her daughter's hand.

'Nice to have met you,' I call, as they waft away like two spirits, down into the forest. I turn back to the platform. This six-year-old knows she's safe because she hasn't yet experienced the opposite. I have had reasons to feel unsafe, and yet, should I be controlled by them? I shouldn't. I grasp the railing and begin easing myself along, crablike, counting the steps to help me concentrate. There are only a dozen, a short distance but a huge leap for me. Raising my head, I look out over the canyon. The mountains are slightly blurred but other than that, symptoms are minimal. I don't feel as if the platform is about to disintegrate around me. In fact, I know it's not. I'm safe; all is well. It's a long way down, though, and a few seconds, this time, is enough. I wish I could tell the little girl how brave I am.

***

Only two cars are parked in the main street of Waratah. Coming from Melbourne, it's surreal to be in a place where there's no traffic – or people, for that matter. It's a bit like one of those science fiction movies where most of life gets killed off by a nuclear explosion, and a few survivors spend their time trying not to get killed by a band of mutants that only come out at night. I'm expecting Charlton Heston to come striding down the street at any moment, sub-machine gun at the ready. It's spotless, though. The lawns in front of the Bischoff Hotel where I'm again booked in for the night, are perfectly mown, so there's someone looking after the town; just not today. The door to the Bischoff is locked. There's a 'For Sale' sign out the front. Have they closed down and forgotten to tell me?

'They'll be back soon,' says the woman in the *Scenic View Cafe*, next door. 'Lewis sliced his hand open so she's taken him to the hospital.' Lewis is the young man who showed me around last time. I hope he's okay. I order a coffee and a slice of quiche. A group of four women sit at a table, swapping local gossip with each other and the woman behind the counter, giving the place a very homey, relaxed feel. It's rather like my brother's cafe on the Great Ocean Road, where the same group of mums come in each morning for their coffee and catch-up.

Old photos from the days of the Mt. Bischoff Mine show a very vibrant place, the main street rimmed with shops and businesses. Two hotels, the Waratah and the Bischoff, sat next to each other. That must have made for some decent competition. Most of the shops have now gone. Mining towns have a life and then fade back into the ground. Maybe that's what's happening here. I climb the hill behind the hotel to what was the vibrantly colourful, spotless school. Weeds have taken over much of the garden and pathways. Paint is peeling off walls and fascias. It's a weekday but there's no-one around. Obviously, it's closed. How incredibly sad. It was one of the loveliest schools I've seen.

Waratah's brochures advertise a tour of the mine but it's no longer on. 'The mine is closed,' says the guide at the *Waratah Museum*.

'That's interesting, because it says on the 'web' it's been reopened.'

'It was for a year, to feed *Rennison Bell*, the tin mine at Rosebury, but they closed it again. We don't know what's happening with it, now.' I've already had a quick look around and am about to escape but he blocks my way. 'There's loads of mining going on around here,' he says. 'Most people don't know about it.'

'Is that right?'

'Yes, there's Hellyer, for zinc and lead.' Not my beautiful Hellyer Gorge, surely! 'No, not the Gorge. Hellyer, a different place. Savage River, for magnetite, the main ore of iron, *Rennison Bell* for tin and, of course, copper at Mt. Lyell in Queenstown.'

He guides me through a maze of memorabilia, including an original poker machine and an incredibly ugly, but mind-bogglingly brilliant, mirror frame, intricately carved by one of the original German families, into tanned wallaby hide. Now *that's* something you don't often see. There's a whole room of minerals and crystals, dug up or found above ground around the area.

'In its heyday,' he continues, '3000 people worked in and around Mt. Bischoff. It was a long way from the mine to the shops and hotels of the town, and so they built a tunnel straight through, to cut down on the time it took to get here.' Of course, they would have; they were miners. The tunnel must have been a very interesting place after closing time. I'm sure the trip took a lot longer going back than coming.

The front door bell jangles and he leaves me to greet his new visitors. The museum is in what was the old court house and council chambers. I love old court rooms, with the warmth of their beautiful polished timber panelling. They take me back to the stories of Charles Dickens: *A Tale of Two Cities, Oliver Twist, Bleak House*; very romantic, though if you were in the dock, 'romantic' wouldn't be the word you'd be using.

'I'm booked in here for the night,' I say to the shy young man who has taken Lewis's spot at the bar of the hotel. He hands me my key and explains how to find my room. It's the same one as last time, next to the bathroom, and I have that feeling of being somewhere familiar and comforting.

If I was expecting the dining experience of last time, a brightly-lit bistro, sparkling with laughing, generous people, which I was, I'm sorely disappointed. The room is empty, except for two couples together at one table. The walls are covered in a very dark brown laminated wood panelling, turning the long, narrow room into a cave. I don't remember that. The large, flat screen television, on which I watched the *Caulfield Cup*, has been replaced by an ugly silver contraption, moved into the corner. The lighting is so dim I can hardly read the menu. The group on the other table ignores me. I plough through my meal and return to the bedroom, rearrange the power points to plug in the electric blanket and sink into the little bed. It's been a good day. I wasn't tired and so achieved everything I wanted with ease. It's definitely worth paying extra to get a good night's sleep in a cabin.

***

'Has the bistro at the hotel been renovated?' I ask the woman in the cafe, as I order my morning 'flat white'.

'No,' she says, 'it hasn't been renovated for years.'

'Oh, right, because I'm sure that panelling wasn't there the last time I was here. It's *very dark*.'

'Yes, it was. It's always been there. They're asking a million and a quarter for it. There's no way they'll get it.' She turns to the same table of women that were here yesterday and they agree. 'No way,' says one, scornfully. Not a lot of love lost between these locals and the owners of the hotel – the parents, that is, not lovely Lewis, surely. A couple seat themselves at the table next to me. They natter together as they decide what they'll have. I pick up their accent – a hobby of mine – from a trip I did to the UK in the 80s. She notices me listening.

'You're from England,' I say, 'from the north?'

'We're from Manchester, originally, but we've been here 40 years.'

'Are you £10 Poms?' Risky; some Poms don't like the question – or being called Poms. Luckily, they don't mind.

'No, just missed out, but we were coming anyway. We had friends in Adelaide so we settled there.' It's their second time touring around Tassie. 'We love it here. We especially love the west.' She chatters about where they've been and where they're heading while her husband sits quietly, nodding and smiling.

'Would you like to see our vehicle?' he suddenly asks.

'Yes,' she says, 'come and have a look at our van.' I gulp the last of my coffee and follow them out. She points to an old, red *Australia Post* van, parked at the kerb. 'We've converted it. It has everything we need.' I love checking out 'homes away from home'. One day I'll have one. I stick my nose through the doorway.

'Do you mind?'

'Sure,' she says. 'Climb in.' Two beds, his across the back, hers along the side and a kitchenette; that's about it. Not a lot of space if they have a tiff and one is giving the other the silent treatment.

'You must get on well together.'

'Well,' she says, her chin lifting proudly, 'we've been married for 50 years.' He nods again and smiles warmly at her. He's hardly got a word in since we met but he doesn't seem to mind, content to sit in the background and listen. The old adage, 'opposites attract', works well in this case.

I wander along the track between barbed-wire-topped fences to the mine. A sign, DANGER, NO ENTRY AUTHORISED PERSONNEL ONLY, hangs from the wire, adding an ominous feel to an already cheerless aspect. Most of the mountain is gone, carved down to a flat, grey and orange moonscape. Low shrubs cling to terraces, in a desperate bid to survive and replace what's been destroyed. It's a sad sight and I've got an awful feeling it will now come back to me every time I open a tin can.

It's hard to know what to make of Waratah. It's certainly not like any town I've known. Something about the west, rather than other beautiful parts of Tassie, draws me and this little town in particular. Maybe it's the spirit of survival, or maybe just that they've got a waterfall in the main street. This plaque could help to explain it: "The township of Waratah did not die alongside its long-term lifeblood, the Mt. Bischoff mine … Timber and forestry provided alternative employment for the ex-miners in the area and new ventures such as the Savage River iron mine in the late 1960s boosted the area's population and economic viability. The township has struggled through some bleak times but the character remains, as it poises now for a new lease of life as tourist numbers begin to increase with the growing appreciation of the rich mining heritage." Here's hoping.

Chapter 23

Again, it's funny how you see things when you're under stress. On my first trip, the road through the bald hills on the way out of Queenstown was narrow, with nothing to stop me going over the edge. I now realise it's the normal width, with quite a strong-looking fence. I had my eyes shut a lot of the time so I guess I missed that. I've had a lot of experience driving around mountains since then. I drove through the Southern Alps to Milford Sound in New Zealand's South Island, following advice from a local that it was easy. I've found out since that most people take a tour, though, given the choice, I would still feel much safer in a sedan than a massive tourist bus. I followed one through the Homer Tunnel and I still don't know how it stayed on the road. And, then, how do you know the bus driver is concentrating? What if he's had a fight with his wife, or his girlfriend – or both? I would rather rely on my lack of concentration that someone else's.

And so I can do this – and I do, with almost no palm-sweating, breath-holding or eye-bulging. I pull off into a wide parking bay halfway up to look around me. I thought it was only in the vicinity of the town that the vegetation was depleted but I'm surrounded by mile after mile of bare orange hills. I could be on another planet. It's horrifying what humans can do to the earth when not thinking. Now and then I sneak a peek as I cover the last two kilometres of roadway and ease back into the forests and valleys of the Lyell Highway. I'm pretty pleased with myself. My fear of heights is on the way to becoming a thing of the past.

I was going to bypass Nelson Falls to allow more time further on but it's impossible. It was here I had my first encounter with a Tasmanian wallaby, though she showed no interest whatever in my existence. The stream rattles over dams created by rocks and the build up of branches and forest matter. The soft shadows envelop me. It's a divine place, gentle and nurturing. There are pixies here, fairies and Elementals. Spirits dip in and out of the waterfall. The wallaby chooses to ignore me again, this time staying out of sight.

***

Ever since the early 1980s, in the days of the Franklin River campaign, I've been intending to come here to see why so many people from so many walks of life spent months in rain and mud, in tents, up trees and in front of bulldozers. I wanted to see what it was they were saving. The river surges past me, wild and free, as it has for millennia. Enormous trees tower around and above me and velvet moss transforms everything into a world of emerald green. I send a silent thank you to them all.

***

I'm booked in tonight at a bush pub, around the corner from the entry to Mt. Field National Park. As usual, I'm excited to see what I'll get *and* a little nervous as to how it will turn out. The *National Park Hotel* was built in 1920 as a boarding house. In 1923, a licence was issued and the building extended. Set into a hollow at the side of the road, it has the look of an Australian homestead, one-storey, white, bordered on two sides by a large veranda. Two men stand smoking outside a heavy, forbidding door. They look at me, surprised, as if I shouldn't be there.

'I'm booked in here for tonight,' I say.

'Oh, alright. Leon's inside.' Leon also looks surprised.

'I'm booked in here tonight.' Every man at the long bar turns and stares.

'I'll get my wife,' says Leon, and disappears through a doorway, leaving me to the men. This used to be intimidating. In my younger days I would have glared back at them, to make the point that things have changed, women are now allowed in bars, and I have as much right as them to be there. But I'm past all that now. Leon returns. 'She's coming.' His wife appears and gestures me to follow. She takes off up a very long, very dark, passageway and I rush after her.

'This is yours,' she says, at the far end, opening a door to a pretty bedroom. Heavy floral and lace curtains line a window overlooking a garden. The walls are rose pink and the bedspread is a soft teal. In the corner are a sink, and a towel and soap.

'The only thing about this room,' she says, 'is that it hasn't got a heater. Do you still want it?' I don't think quickly at any time, let alone when I've been on the road for hours. 'I can give you a different one,' she urges, but she doesn't want to.

'Umm, is there an electric blanket?'

'Oh yes, of course there's an electric blanket.'

'Should be alright, then.'

'I'll show you the bathroom.' She dashes away and I follow in her wake, trying hard to keep up. The bathroom is as far away from my room as it can be without actually being outside. No sneaking next door in my tee shirt in the middle of the night here. She takes off again and leads me to a large breakfast room attached to a very cosy lounge, a log fire already burning in the grate, a television in the corner.

'Cereal and milk, bread for the toaster.'

'Fabulous.'

'This is *your* spot.' She stands next to a table against the wall, where cutlery and crockery have been laid out and covered with a linen cloth. I immediately want to move them to a different spot. It's a flaw I have when confronted with rigid rules. I wonder what would happen if I did. Sent to bed without dinner? *I will do as I am told,* one hundred times on the blackboard?

'Where are you parked,' she asks. I wave my arm.

'Outside somewhere ... in a car park.' At this stage, I'm completely disoriented. She opens a door and points to my car.

'You can use this door but it *has* to be locked once you're in. Okay?'

'Okay.'

'Dinner is between 6.30 and 8.00.' I nod and she's gone.

It's 4 o'clock. I wander out through the bar – I don't dare open the back door in case it won't close again – and out into the car park. The hotel is not totally in the bush as I expected. A few houses are scattered along each side of the road. I find my way through some scrub to a stream bordered by an old railway line and sit on a stump. The sounds of the bush, the droning of bees and mosquitoes, the chirping of tiny birds and the rippling of the water, relax me. Tomorrow, I'm taking this road down to see the famous tall trees of the Styx Valley. I've asked Leon about the 15 kilometres of gravel road leading into the valley and he assures me my car will handle it.

***

Cheery voices and laughter emanate from the dining room. A log fire has been lit and it is no longer the dark, cold space I passed through three hours ago. Leon is behind the counter, serving the bar on one side and the dining room on the other, along with taking orders for food. It takes some patience but I eventually order my meal, along with a *Shiraz* Leon insists is beautiful and I have to try. Leon's idea of a beautiful *Shiraz* and mine are two different things; not that I know the first thing about wines, but I know what tastes good and what doesn't. I finish it, though – it's not *that* bad. A large family, three generations, sprawls either side of a long table and a group of four takes up a corner. A young woman sits alone in the middle of the room, her head down over a book. I'm not the only single staying here, then. She's probably around 30, and I wish I could find out what she's doing here. I expect she's come for the forests – you wouldn't find yourself here by accident. It's a detour from the main highway so a decision is required. I look up half way through my meal to find she's disappeared.

***

The car rattles along the last of the gravel road into the car park of Styx Valley Reserve. There are no other cars so I may have the place to myself for a while. 'Daylight Saving' ended last night and I expect everyone is taking advantage of the extra hour to sleep in. I park beside an archway created by giant ferns, seducing me to peer through. Rotted tree trunks, covered in rotting leaves and moss, are sinking, bit by bit, back into the earth. Large trees with tiny leaves loom up out of the dimness of the forest floor and zoom into glimpses of pale blue sky. Birds twitter and a there's a strange buzzing I can't quite identify, underlying it all. It's another realm, a bit medieval. I roamed through here as a child with the Brothers Grimm. I half expect to see a line of little white pebbles left by Hansel and Gretel. I choose not to enter, afraid I might disappear down a rabbit hole, Alice-like, into a parallel world.

I cross the road onto a walking track and up a hill. Something is following alongside me. It takes a minute to realise it's the trunk of a fallen tree, but not like any tree I've ever seen. Its girth is enormous. I look behind me to find its root base but all I can see is trunk. In front of me, the same thing. The tree is so long I can't see where it begins and where it ends. It's then that I look up. I came to see tall trees but I had no concept of how tall they were actually going to be. One of these eucalypts has been measured at 92metres; that's a 25 storey building.

I sit for a while, goggle-eyed, at the massive base, some five metres around, of one of these giants. A sign explains:

Their incredible size is due to their efficiency in moving water and nutrients through a central tube known as xylern, in a way that's a bit like drinking through a straw. Brilliant. *As the trees age, the flow declines, causing death of, at first, the upper limbs and later, the whole tree.* Not unlike humans. *Gradual rotting of the base makes the trees vulnerable to collapse under their enormous weight, along with storm-force winds. Decomposing trees add to the nutrient-rich soil.*

Back at the car, a sign points to a track through the forest to the river. It's a pleasant, easy walk, until the track narrows and all but disappears and I'm fighting my way through scrub, low tree branches scraping my face and dragging at my hair. It's with a touch of relief that I hear the rippling of the rusty water. These waters are coloured a reddish-brown by tannins, leached from the button grass plains of the *World Heritage* areas. There's a rumour that the name of the river was inspired by Greek Mythology, the River Styx being the boundary between the Earth and the Underworld of Hades. It was so respected by the gods, that they would take binding oaths just by mentioning its name. If a god gave his oath and failed to keep his word, Zeus would force him to drink from the river. The water was so foul he would lose his voice for nine years.

Nothing so menacing in this lovely spot. The trees here are smaller, less regal – gentler: dogwood, myrtle and sassafras. Dead branches and tree trunks litter the river bank. I sit on a log at the river's edge and breathe in the cool, pure air. Two brown and grey robins bounce around me, picking under the leaves at my feet as if I wasn't there. I brush at a mosquito and they dart away. The cackle of a kookaburra ripples gently, rising in a crescendo of joy and triumph, then ebbs, eerily, back into the forest.

Chapter 24

I haven't driven into Hobart's centre before. Last time, I left the car in its spot in the holiday park on the other side of the river. I'm anxious about getting lost or tangled up in traffic but the freeway leads straight into Davey Street and one right-hand turn takes me to my digs. It's a modern hotel and, as is the way these days, the room is very small. This is okay, except that the only place for my case is between the bed and window. I don't know how couples manage to move around. On the bright side, it's only four steps from the bed to the toilet.

I race to the jug to replenish myself with coffee and find that the power point is already taken up by the lamp and the fridge. I could unplug the lamp but that would mean putting the jug on the floor because its cord is too short to reach from the desk. There's a power point in the bathroom but I make a further inspection of the bedroom, knowing that modern hotel rooms have to allow for a myriad of gadgets. There *is* one on either side of the bed, used for lamps, and so my choice is thus: plug the jug in on the floor, on a bedside table or squeezed in beside the bathroom sink. I choose the sink.

I'm here for three nights and while the water is boiling I decide to hang up a few clothes. There's a small cupboard to hang them in but no coat hangers. I know this place was cheap for the middle of a city, a mere $120 a night, but that's no reason not to have a few coat hangers – or an extra power point. And the toilet smells – badly. Am I a whinger? I'm on a roll so I may as well finish. There's a lift to the basement car park but at the moment it's not going to the basement. If you want something out of the car, you catch the lift to the ground floor, walk along the street and down into the car park, get what you want, walk back up the street to the ground floor and catch the lift back to your room.

The sun is shining but the wind blasts at me, reminding me of my own windy city. It's with relief that I'm leaving the car in its spot and spending the next couple of days on foot. I can't say I enjoyed Hobart the last time I was here. It seemed a bleak place in the middle of winter but it's very pretty now, with the sunshine glowing in the golden stone of the beautiful old buildings. My hotel is in a good spot, one block from St. David's Park, on the other side of which are the Criminal Courts, Parliament House and Salamanca Place. Everything seems to be placed in a circle around the docks: the Town Hall, Art Gallery and *Theatre Royal* are all within a couple of blocks. I have various plans – a harbour cruise, a visit to *Cascades Female Factory* and an exploration of Battery Point. I set out down the first of Hobart's many steep hills toward St. David's Park. Let's hope the aroma from the toilet has dissipated when I get back or it's going to be a long night.

***

The room was as sweet as a daisy when I returned. Whatever was in there had crawled back to its nether world. I'm waiting at Franklin Square for a bus to take me to the *Cascade Female Factory*. Women convicts, on the whole, haven't had the press of the men, and so I'm surprised to learn that over 13,000 women were transported to Van Diemen's Land between 1803 and the cessation of transportation in 1853. The earliest to Hobart were kept in a dilapidated building attached to the city gaol, where they slept in two unventilated rooms. All classes mixed together, from those awaiting trial for murder to those transported for stealing a hanky. With nothing to do all day but wander around the yard, it followed that the innocent were corrupted by the guilty. The gaol at Launceston was in an even worse condition, in that the prisoners could not all lie down at the same time but had to take turns in lying down and standing up. Obviously, the British Government had given no thought to women when they designed their system.

George Arthur arrived in 1824 with the idea of taking control of this errant island colony and pulling it into shape. To solve the problem of overcrowding of the women, he bought a rum distillery, a mile and a half from town, and had it converted into a prison and workhouse. I leave the bus and follow a sign down a side street, past pretty cottages and across a bridge over a stream. Fifteen foot stone walls rise before me.

'The tour goes for an hour and a quarter,' says the young woman at the counter.

'An hour and a quarter? Can I do it on my own?'

'Well, yes, you can but there are very few buildings left.'

'I hadn't realised that.'

'Yes, so the tour is necessary, you know, to get the full story.' I'm a bit uncomfortable tied down to tours, especially for that length of time. Once you're in, it's hard to get away.

'I'll wander by myself to start with, see how I go.'

'No charge, then,' she says. She hands me a brochure showing me the original layout of the prison. It sat in a dark valley in the foothills of Mt. Wellington. If I had entered the large double gate in 1829, I would have encountered a labyrinth of stone dividing walls as high as the outer wall, enclosing workrooms, dormitories, nursery, hospital, offices, store rooms and officers' quarters. The ground was also paved with stone, making it difficult for water to run off and so, with little light filtering past the walls, it must have been a wet, cold and demoralising place.

The inmates were separated into three classes: *Crime*, with low rations and severe punishment, *Probation*, with extra food and milder punishment, and *Assignable*, women able to be sent outside the walls to work for settlers. This could be a dicey proposition, as many of them returned pregnant. Pregnancy was evidence of unauthorised behaviour and so a crime, and punished accordingly, often in the solitary cells. Nothing was ever asked of the men or the circumstances. The babies were weaned at nine months, at which time the mothers went back to the bottom of the ladder in *Crime* Class to start all over again. They rarely saw their children after that. The toddlers lived in the nursery, four to a cot, and, I assume, got their sustenance from each other. Not enough, though. With the constant damp and cold and the heat in summer, along with the lack of any nurturing, a great many took the easier option of dying. At three, those that survived were placed in orphanages.

In December 1832, a petition signed, 'Nursery Women', begged Governor Arthur, who personally controlled everything in the colony, to give them an extra six months with their babies after they were weaned: "we will take care for the future,' they wrote, 'as none of us that is now in came in for a sentence only the crime of being pregnant and the first time and that it will be the last..." The women pleaded "not to treat us as objects of guilt but pity us." To no avail; Arthur stuck to his guns, 'approving of the regulations being strictly enforced except in very special cases.' I wonder how cases could be more special than these.

In the centre of the yard, a series of plaques describes the development of the prison and the lives of a few of the inmates, most of whom weren't criminals but victims of the poverty of their times. The gaol grew as more and more ships poured their cargo into the colony. The second yard, opened in 1832, contained 100 solitary confinement cells, a slight case of overkill, I would have thought, as there were only 324 inmates at the time. The original cells were six feet by four, built into the main wall, with little or no ventilation and no light to allow the women to occupy themselves in any way. These later cells were considered 'roomy' and 'well-ventilated', being around eleven feet by four, with a small, barred opening over the outer door to let in some light. This allowed a woman to work at spinning or sewing, thereby not being quite the victim of her mind as she would have been in total darkness.

The normal sentence was one week but it was often extended to two. The public demanded that 'depraved' women be severely dealt with and yet treated humanely, and so solitary confinement was considered more humane than the floggings allotted to the men. Charles Dickens disagreed. As a member of the anti-solitary confinement lobby in England, he wrote: "I hold this slow and daily tampering with the mysteries of the brain to be immeasurably worse than torture of the body, because its ghastly signs and tokens are not so palpable to the eye and sense of touch as scars upon the flesh; because its wounds are not upon the surface and it exhorts few cries that human ears can hear."

Not all of the women were submissive and orderly and a special form of punishment was reserved for those. This was a band of iron, about an inch and a half thick, which opened at the back to clasp around the neck and fastened at the front with a padlock. From this collar projected four iron spikes, about a foot long, tapering to sharp points. The whole weight of the iron rested on the collarbones of the woman. The term for wearing the collar was from 24 to 60 hours. The worst insult of all, though, for the women of the *Crime* Class and those sent to solitary, was the shaving of their hair. They could stand anything but the loss of their much-valued locks, and often became hysterical as the dreaded shears approached.

Still, many made the most of their situation and never returned after being assigned. They remained with their first master until they became eligible for a 'Ticket of Leave', which allowed them to move around a designated district. A Conditional Pardon meant they could go anywhere but the British Isles. I can't imagine there'd be many wanting to risk the British Isles again. A few eventually regained complete freedom of movement when granted a Free Pardon, married and their descendants live in Tassie today.

***

I'm not sure what the bus driver was on, but we were back in town in about three minutes flat. In fact, I didn't realise we'd arrived until he told me I had to get off. It's a short walk down Elizabeth Street to the docks. Expensive-looking, white yachts, dozens of them, bob in the grey ripples of the marina, straining a little at their moorings as if waiting for their chance to get away. This is the finishing line for the annual Sydney to Hobart Yacht Race; yachting is huge here.

Hobart has a fascinating history. With the confirmation by Flinders and Bass that Van Diemen's Land was an island, the British claim to the east coast of Australia was not legally valid here. The French had been exploring the area for years and since the Napoleonic Wars had broken out, Governor King sent a request to London for permission to send someone down fast, to prevent the French from establishing a naval base. Sick of waiting for a reply he acted on his own initiative. He sent 23-year-old Lieutenant John Bowen, in charge of the whaler, *Albion*, with 21 male and three female convicts, guarded by marines of the *New South Wales Corp* and a small number of free settlers. The supply ship, the *Lady Nelson,* followed. They set themselves up at Risdon Cove, on the eastern side of the river.

In the meantime, David Collins, a Lieutenant in *Syrius*, on the first fleet 15 years earlier and, for a time, Judge Advocate of the new colony, had been dispatched in answer to King's request and immediately took command. Changing tides and poor water supply caused him to look around for an alternative location. He settled on Sullivans Cove for its sheltered, deep water harbour, allowing easy access for shipping. A fresh water supply came from Hobart Rivulet, which flows down from Mt. Wellington into the Derwent River. The company landed in February, 1804, making Hobart the second established city in Australia.

It was soon realised that the island's isolation could prove useful as a secondary penal colony. Port Jackson's growing convict population was becoming difficult to manage and it was decided to break it up into smaller groups, sending some to Norfolk Island and others to Van Diemen's Land. That's the decision that determined the dark road Tasmania would take for the next 50 years. Without that decision, what would the colony have been? From the beginning free settlers were arriving, searching for somewhere to make a fresh start. Left to itself, it would surely have developed naturally, a place of peace and beauty, without the burden of shame inherent in being an island prison. Progress would have been slower, no doubt, without the free labour of the convicts but it would have happened. On the other hand, some shame would still have been carried, though felt more in the future than then, when at last the disastrous results of white settlement on the indigenous peoples were understood.

Mark Twain visited Hobart in 1897 and wrote: "How beautiful is the whole region, for form and grouping and opulence, and freshness of foliage and variety of colour, and grace and shapeliness of the hills, the capes, the promontories; and then, the splendour of the sunlight, the dim, rich distances, the charm of the water glimpses! And it was in this paradise that the yellow-liveried convicts were landed, and Corps-bandits quartered, and the wanton slaughter of the kangaroo-chasing black innocents consummated on that autumn day in May, in the brutish old time. It was all out of keeping with the place, a sort of bringing of heaven and hell together."

***

I'm looking forward to relaxing back on a ferry ride around the bay. 'Sorry,' says the woman behind the desk at *Captain Fell's Harbour Cruises*, 'you're the only one. We need a few more to go out.'

'Right. Do you think more will come?' Why am I asking her that? How would she know?

'No idea,' she says. 'You could come back in an hour and check.' She's hoping to get off early, I can tell.

'Thanks, maybe next time.'

The *Sea Shepherd* is in dock, back, no doubt, from chasing Japanese whalers around the southern ocean. Its hull is painted in war-like colours and huge shark's teeth decorate its bow. It's logo is a type of skull and crossbones. These young sailors go to war against a perceived enemy. I'm past believing that conflict achieves anything, though, at their age, I would have been all for it. They're fund-raising and I slink past to avoid them. Further along the pier is a sailing ship. It's the replica of Captain Cook's *Endeavour*, on its last day in Hobart. You can be lucky; plans fall apart to be replaced by something better. Nine dollars gets me on the tour and into heaven. I stand on the deck, imagining myself blown by the winds from one exotic place to another – a good dream, considering with my history of sea-sickness, I would have been dead the first day out. The ship was launched in 1993, and has been sailing the world since.

Sailing ships were the epitome of organisation. There was a place for everything and I wonder what would have happened to the person who forgot to put something back. Keelhauled, perhaps. There were 85 men on the ship with Cook. Working, sleeping and eating were done in shifts and anyone wanting privacy would've chosen a different career. Hammocks are strung along the walls to show where the sailors slept. Officers shared cabins. It must have been a challenge for the cook to produce meals every day for so many in the tiny space that was the galley; that, and the fact that he had only one arm. It's true; he had only one arm.

We enter the Great Cabin where Cook worked and dined, sharing the space with botanist, Joseph Banks. I could be in an episode of *Hornblower*, or with Russell Crowe in *Master and Commander*, or any BBC production with sailing ships. I pop my head into Cook's and Banks' cabins. Although they were definitely head and shoulders, so to speak, above what the crew had, they were still a tight fit, considering both men were well over six foot. Joseph Banks was six foot four, and so often slept in a swing cot slung in the Great Cabin, leaving his space to his pets.

On the way back I look in on the little Catholic Church opposite my hotel. Having just explored beautiful *St. David's Anglican Cathedral*, I'm surprised at how small and nondescript *St. Joseph's* is. There's none of the theatricality you usually get. I think it's the first Catholic Church I've ever seen without a central aisle and, in fact, it doesn't look like a Catholic Church at all. There's a man doing the 'Stations of the Cross' and as I leave, he rushes out after me.

'Have you wondered why Jesus led you to this church?' he asks.

'He led me to a few others on the way.' Did I say that aloud or just think it? A bit mean either way but I was caught by surprise. He doesn't notice.

'Yes, but to *this* church ... today?' meaning, no doubt, when he was here. He advises me of the sad fact of my being born in sin, which I already knew because the nuns told me. 'Humans always take the sinful option,' he says, 'don't they?'

'Do we?'

'Well,' he says, surprised at the question, 'we do, don't we?'

'That's a bit insulting. I think I'm quite a nice person a lot of the time.'

'No, no,' he says, 'but it's true.'

'I don't think so.' I wave my arm at the streets around us. 'Look at these people. They're just going about their business. No-one's doing anything horrible.' This stops him in his tracks, probably not an idea he's been presented with before, but only for a moment.

'Yes, but the Devil is always looking for a chance to tempt us.'

'I don't think I believe in the Devil, anymore.' He's shocked – and really worried for me. I soften. I was brought up Catholic, with the same 'father-child', 'reward-punishment', system, and so I do know where he's coming from. Further discussion ensues which, of course, gets us nowhere.

'I'll be fine,' I say, eventually. 'You can say a prayer for me.' This is to allay his anxiety, but he looks so sad as I escape up the street that I think he's given my Soul up as a lost cause.

***

The sun is again shining off the water and the sky is a vibrant blue as I enter the park. Lunchtime in Franklin Square is a very civilised affair. Office workers loll on park benches under the oak trees, seagulls strut on the lawns, alert for anything that might be dropped and children bounce around the large fountain, squealing as they're sprayed by the water spouts. Rising from the centre of the fountain is the statue of Sir John Franklin. John was the nephew of Matthew Flinders. Matthew grew up in the village of Donnington in Lincolnshire and the Franklins lived nearby in Spilsby. Flinders took young John on the *Investigator* as a midshipman and so instigated his exploring career. After serving in the Napoleonic Wars, he was chosen to lead an expedition to chart the north coast of Canada. Eleven of his 20 men died of starvation.

In 1825, he returned to the Arctic to explore the Beaufort Sea. This expedition was better supplied and more successful. He was knighted by *George IV* on 29th April, 1829. In the meantime, he'd married Jane Griffin, a friend of his first wife who had died of tuberculosis.

Jane was liberated for a woman of her day and, as a seasoned traveller, suited him perfectly. In 1836, Sir John was appointed Lieutenant-Governor of Van Diemen's Land, following the recall of George Arthur. It was a difficult job for all the Governors, who spent much of their time trying to hold onto their power against the obstruction of land owners and the town's officials, who were often as corrupt as the convicts.

Franklin's humane views were not appreciated. He saw religion as a reforming influence and subsidised all of the religious denominations. The amount depended on the size of the congregation and so there was quite a bit of unseemly raiding of others' flocks on the part of the pastors, to win a bigger subsidy. He set up the island's first primary schools, excluding the creed, catechism and doctrine from the curriculum in favour of simple bible reading. This upset Francis Nixon, the first Anglican bishop of Van Diemen's Land, who described Franklin's schools as "monstrous, unsound and unsafe ... education would virtually be that of the infidel. I'd rather see my children die than go to one of them."

Along with that, he and Jane were not averse to 'roughing it'. They became lost in the wilderness on a trek between Hobart and Strahan and lives were lost during their rescue. This further distanced the couple from 'proper' society. Even so, they were popular with the people of Tasmania. By the time they were recalled in 1843, they had founded *Christ College*, the Tasmanian Museum and the Art Gallery, among many other institutions and societies, culminating in Hobart becoming incorporated as a city in 1842. If you ask me, they were a fabulous couple.

Franklin's second expedition to the Arctic had left less than 500 kilometres of unexplored coastline. He was sent to complete the job, even though at that stage he was 59 years of age. The expedition set sail in May, 1845 and was last seen by Europeans in July of that year. On the plinth below the statue appears an epitaph, written by Alfred Lord Tennyson, Sir John's nephew:

> *Not here! The white north hath thy bones and thou*
> *Heroic sailor soul*
> *Art passing on thine happier voyage now*
> *Toward no earthly pole*

***

Battery Point is perched on a cliff overlooking Salamanca Place and the docks. During colonial times, this area was a colourful maritime village, home to master mariners, shipwrights, sailors and merchants. To cut down on time and save walking all the way around the point, shipwright and adventurer, Captain James Kelly, built steps down, creating a short cut from the gentrification of the cottages on the hill, to the decidedly less gentrified region of the docks, warehouses, pubs and general goings-on of Wapping. Very sensible. I, for one, am grateful. I'm determined not to let Hobart's hills wear me down but at this stage the hills are winning.

The steps take me up to Kelly Street and along to Hampden Road. Tiny bluestone cottages, like little boxes, their front doors opening directly onto the street, vie for space with sandstone mansions, chimneys sprouting from their steep slate roofs, their gardens framed by lacy, wrought-iron fences. Gas street lamps stand at intervals along the pavements. I could be back in the 1800s. I half expect Governor Arthur to trot past me on his trusty steed, followed by his ever-present, young aide-de-camp, his nephew, Charles Arthur.

Arthur Circus is a circle of quaint little cottages built around a village green. In 1829, the Governor, having, as usual, his finger in every pie, bought the land from Reverend Robert Knopwood, who seemed, at the time, to own half of Hobart. When he sold it 20 years later, the auction advertisement described "delectable building sites in a neighbourhood that will inevitably become The Resort of the Beau Monde." Pretty right there. Location is everything, they say. I can only imagine what one of these properties would cost. There's not much in the way of shops, though. Maybe they just pop down to Salamanca Place for their needs, which is something, if it was offered to me (at about half the going rate), I wouldn't knock back.

At the top end of the street is *Narryna Heritage Museum*. *Narryna* was built in 1836 by Captain Andrew Haig, who had a mind to make a killing in the new colony. He arrived in 1824 with a ship load of cargo from India. With the money from the sale, he bought two acres of land from, again, Reverend Knopwood. "This place is in a very flourishing condition," he wrote, "and will no double (sic) become of much importance ... There is considerable trade carried on between this and Port Jackson in wheat, the colony being peculiarly adapted for the growth of that article ... Every ship from England brings out a great number of settlers who generally bring dollars with them so there is no want of specie."

Captain Haig was not one of the entrepreneurs who prospered in the new colony. In 1842, during the economic depression of the time, he was forced to sell all his property, including a warehouse in Salamanca Place and *Narryna*. It's had many incarnations since, as a rental property for many years, a boarding house and an after-care hospital for female tuberculosis patients. The *Tasmanian Research Society*, the *Shiplovers Society of Tasmania* and the *Battery Point Progress Association*, got together and requested it be preserved and so it became Australia's first heritage museum.

I'm so glad. This is as close as I'll ever get to the 1830s, in particular to the clothes worn by the women. I've seen these dresses, needless to say, in virtually every period drama that comes on television, but up this close I can see every stitch, every bit of lace and embroidery; every tuck and frill. Day dresses, ball gowns, children's clothes and a wedding dress. It's a fantastic display. The poor women, though, were trussed up like chickens. I'm not surprised they fainted away at the drop of a hat.

I wander past a strange-looking, tall, narrow chair. A sign perches on the seat:

Posture Chair (1830). The posture or correction chair designed by Sir Astley Cooper (1768-1841) to improve the deportment of the young child. The small seat, high legs and straight back forced the child to sit upright or to topple off. Good deportment was very important in the Victorian era as it was considered a sign of good breeding. It was a tough life for the children.

The main bedroom contains two rather brilliant and exceedingly upmarket versions of commodes. One is disguised as the bottom drawer of a chest of drawers;

the other is a version of bedside steps. The pot is hidden in a compartment at the top of the steps and drawn out onto the second step when needed. The person stands on the bottom step and releases himself onto the pot. When finished, the pot goes back to its hiding place. It's certainly a very elegant spin on the old 'chamber pot under the bed' trick. *Narryna* doesn't get the press of some of the more well-known heritage estates – I'd never heard of it before picking up a brochure from the tourist centre – but it's as beautiful a presentation as I've seen.

***

I sit on the edge of Princes Park. It's 24°C. Yachts speckle the waters of the Derwent. A child squeals with delight as her mother chases her around the playground behind me. The city hums quietly. I'm very glad I came back for another look at Hobart.

Chapter 25

Shelley Beach at Orford reintroduces me to the east coast. It's much friendlier-looking than it seemed on my first trip when the winter weather was dragging me down. No dragging here. Bass and Flinders must have been constantly stunned by what they were discovering. The long white beach runs along one side of Prosser Bay. Houses have been built looking across to Point Home Lookout on the headland opposite. To the right, in the distance, are the painted cliffs of Maria Island. Two small children run down a sand hill and onto the beach. Their grandfather trudges behind them, followed by a dog, some sort of spaniel, skipping in circles, beside itself with joy. A small boat bobs in the water with two men sitting quietly fishing. A soft breeze is the only movement in the air. It's warm already, leading up to the mid 20s by lunchtime.

Triabunna is where you catch the ferry to the remains of the *Maria Island Penal Settlement*. It's an odd little town, not quite as polished-looking as the other more touristy fishing villages I remember. Very relaxed, I'd say, especially on the roads. A car cuts me off and a motor bike pulls out directly in front of me. Luckily, I'm concentrating well enough to avoid them. I'm not always. A man chugs down the centre of the road in a motorised wheel-chair, a 'don't mess with me' look on his face. I guess the locals know him and keep a watch out.

Spiky Bridge, just south of Swansea, is a strange contraption. Its walls are made from fieldstones laid without mortar, though hundreds of stones have been cemented, vertically, along the tops. This gives the bridge a spiky appearance. It was built after Edward Shaw of *Redbanks* gave Major De Guillume, superintendent of Rocky Hills Probation Station, a ride home one night for a game of piquet. Shaw drove his gig through the gully at full gallop to impress upon the major the need for more road works. Needless to say, the ride was very unpleasant and the bridge was erected shortly afterwards. It's thought that the spikes were designed to prevent cattle falling over the sides but no-one knows for sure. Maybe De Guillume was getting back at Shaw just a little for his rough ride.

***

'I suppose you get used to the view,' I say to the woman behind the reception desk at the Swansea Motor Inn, as I stare out across the expanse of Great Oyster Bay.

'I've been working here 28 years,' she says, 'and I've never got used to it. I go out there with my coffee all the time and just look as different stuff happens. A dog will run on the beach, whatever, I never get used to it.'

The highway through the town is very quiet, none of the Easter and Victorian school holiday traffic I was expecting. I cross to the other side and wander up a hill. *All Saints Anglican Church* and the *Uniting Church of Australia* sit on opposite sides of the road, the manse of the Anglican abutting the Uniting church, with no fence separating them. Maybe they've given in and joined forces. From up here there's a beautiful view of the Freycinet Peninsula. I can understand free settlers choosing this area to start their new lives. Swansea is not unlike English fishing villages, or maybe Welsh, hence the name, with their cottages meandering down the hills to the wharf.

It's late afternoon as I drive down to Schouten Beach. It should be a totally different experience in sunlight, as opposed to the rain and grey of my first visit. The water glitters with pale blue lights. Waves rustle, like car tyres over gravel, in toward the shore, turn in on themselves and then, as if sneaking up and attacking, crash onto the sand. Soft grey and pink clouds scatter the blue sky. By the time I reach the lookout on *Loontitetermairrelorner Track*, the Freycinet is draped in a mauve haze. An almost full, translucent moon hangs over the deep purple peaks of The Hazards, as if suspended from a wire. The sky darkens and the moon becomes brighter. Its rays, sparkling golden in the water, form a perfect pathway to my bench on the hill. Night descends softly onto Great Oyster Bay.

Two campervans are parked along the edge of the beach. A young couple sit at a camp table, eating their dinner by the light of a candle. That's what you can do when you take your accommodation with you – find a stunning spot and set yourself up in the middle of it. I'm going to have to consider a camper van at some stage; I feel like I'm missing out. I'm no spring chicken, though, so I won't want to put it off for too long.

***

The air is cool as I stand at the lookout and gaze across Moulting Lagoon Game Reserve, at the northern end of Great Oyster Bay. The Lagoon holds the largest concentration of black swans in Tasmania, with 8000 to 10,000 living there. The name comes from the shedding of their flight feathers, which can often be seen piled up along the shoreline. The reserve is important as a breeding ground for wetland birds and a destination for migratory birds, as well as for fauna and rare wetland and coastal flora.

Australia is a signatory to the 1971 'Ramsar Convention', an international treaty that deals with conservation and wise use of the world's wetlands. Ramsar is the city in Iran where the treaty was signed. We also have agreements with Japan and China, for the protection of the passage of migratory birds between countries, and the maintenance of their habitats. And so, for all we endlessly hear through the media of threats from other countries, many are going about their business, quietly co-operating with each other.

The area also has important cultural values. At the time of European settlement, it was occupied by the Oyster Bay nation. The majority of bands in this nation used the lagoon on a seasonal basis, while the *Linetemairrener* people lived here all year round. Wildlife, black swan eggs in particular, was an important food source. A vineyard lies in the valley below me and further on, small lakes make up part of the wetlands, leading the eye to the bay and the misty blue Freycinet. Crows call to each other in the light sunshine. The only sound, other than birds, is the odd car on the road behind me. It's one of the most peaceful places I've ever been.

I stop at Scamander and plough down a sand hill onto a beach that seems to go forever. The sun has disappeared behind heavy clouds and the ocean is a greenish-grey. The full force of the wind whips up the waves and sends them crashing and frothing onto the sand, thrashing at clumps of olive green seaweed left their by other waves. The sand is bordered by small cliffs which reach all the way along to a headland in the distance.

I always experience a reality check when standing at the edge of an ocean. It's so huge and I'm so small. It's been around forever and I'm hoping to manage 70 or 80 years. It reminds me that I'm just passing through, which is an idea I'm very comfortable with. It brings the old ego back in check, just for the moment. Everyone should come to places like this – often. We might end up taking the Earth more seriously and giving her a break. I criss-cross my footsteps back to my starting point, offer a little 'thanks', and head back to the car.

I pass through St. Helen's and follow the Tasman Highway away from the coast and into the forests of the Blue Tiers. Not far from Weldborough, where I'm staying at the hotel for the night, is the turnoff to St. Columba Falls, in the fertile George River valley. The valley was opened up to farming by George and Margaret Cotton. In Spring of 1875, with their 10 children, they fought their way on horse and on foot, through 40 kilometres of trackless mountainous wilderness to establish their property. They named it *St. Columba*. I find it hard to get my head around a family of 12 fighting their way through the forest. Did the children take it in their stride? Mine squabbled in the car on the way to the supermarket.

The early pioneers of the North-East had no choice but to be tough. Annie Beachley ran a dairy farm with her husband and six children. In 1908, one of her cows failed to return for milking. She went searching for it in the dense forest behind their property and became lost. A week later, she was given up for dead. After nine days, she appeared near the falls before two startled men. After being taken to the men's home for food and drink, she said, 'If you could take me halfway home, I could walk the other half.'

Annie explained that on the ninth day she came across a creek she had already passed five times and realised she was going round in circles. 'I selected a log on which I thought my friends might find me,' she said, 'and lay down to die … But something seemed to say to me that God would not let me die there. I arose, determined to make one more effort, and this time came onto some grass and two men.' She was stalked by two Tasmanian Tigers for two days, apparently waiting for her to die. One night she slept in a hollow log and found them in the morning, peering in at her from both ends. Annie recovered and was hailed the bravest woman of 1908. Of any time, I would have thought.

***

There's a hole in the window of my room at the Weldborough Hotel. A piece of cardboard covers it, held on by packing tape.

'This is yours,' says Mark, the very friendly proprietor. He doesn't think the hole in the window is worth mentioning or maybe he's forgotten it's there. It's right over the top of my bed so I hope it's well sealed, otherwise I'm going to get a draught of extremely cold Tasmanian night air. It's a very small room, more of a cell, really. These rooms were used by miners, working in shifts at the Weldborough and Derby tin mines. It would have been not unlike Cook's crew on the *Endeavour*. As one lot was leaving, the next was waiting to move in – they slept and left and so space wasn't a priority. Still, there's everything I need: large bed, just squeezing in between the walls, a dressing table and a small coil heater. It's clean and freshly painted and the bathroom is only two doors down.

The highway passes the front of the hotel and disappears into the dark forest. Old cottages line the side of the road, some having been maintained, others definitely not. A man's loud voice echoes from the innards of a house with tin halfway up the outer walls, a reasonable solution to rotting wood. Junk has gathered around the yard and a broken trampoline leans against the wall. Further along, the heart-wrenching tones of Brenda Lee singing *The Biggest Fool of All*, wafts from a dark little bungalow, and next door to that, Hank Williams with *I'm So Lonesome I Could Cry*. It's like being in a time warp. I could be in the back woods of America just as easily as Tassie's north-east.

The dark bar has been transformed while I was out and is now a cheerful dining room, filled with the chatter of parents and their children. The land around the hotel is rented to campers. 'I charge them $5 or $10 for the night,' Mark said, 'or nothing. They can come in here to eat or not. I don't mind.' Some have opted to come in. There's a feeling about this place, as if it's not so much a hotel, as someone's home where people come for a visit. It's not the Ritz but I'm sure a stay at the Ritz wouldn't be this relaxed and friendly. I choose the smallest table. I have a dread, as a single, that I might be getting in the way, taking up space that may be needed by others.

A family enters, parents and three little boys, probably aged four, three and two. The children are treated as if they're the world's most precious beings and they act accordingly, nattering quietly with each other while they wait patiently for their meal. Another family sits nearby, with a little girl, around the age of five. They were in the hotel when I arrived and she has been yelling incessantly since. The parents seem oblivious to her hyper-activity, while her two older brothers sit, strangely silent. I hope she settles down; what with the draught from the window and her noise, I may not get much sleep. The food is lovely and the *Shiraz* even better. Great wine in the back blocks of Tassie.

The girl pounds up the passage, her family following in her wake. They thump around in their room for a while, doing I can't imagine what, and then suddenly all is quiet. I throw aside my book and snuggle under the deliciously warm doona.

***

I wake early to the rustling of trees and the cackling of kookaburras. I have no idea what the situation is around breakfast. Mark said he might set it up in the bistro but he didn't say for sure and he didn't say at what time and

I was too tired to ask for details. I decide to load up the car in preparation for leaving, at which stage others will be up and about and may know what's going on.

There's a sign on the wall next to the light switch, with code numbers for opening the hotel's back door from the outside. I'm not too confident about memorising numbers this early in the morning and anyway, the door stayed open easily enough yesterday. Famous last words. I rush at it as it moves away from me and closes with a sinister clunk. I'm locked out. I bang on various doors and windows around the building to no avail. The hotel is locked up and will stay that way for who knows how long.

You don't want to be caught in the open at 7am in the bitter cold of a Tassie forest, in a light jumper only fit for a 20° day. But there's a solution to all problems. I'll sit in the car. That way, at least, I'll be out of the damp air. There's a heavy windcheater in there. I can be warm as well as dry while I wait for someone to open the door. But how will I know it's been opened if I'm in the car park at the other side of the hotel? There's an old couch on the back patio. I'll sit there and rush for the door when it opens. Ten minutes pass and I'm not a 'happy little Vegemite'. At last, I hear the father and his manic child thumping along the passage and make a dash for the door as they pass through, jamming my fingers in the gap just before it shuts. The ensuing pain is overshadowed by the thrill of being warm again or, at least, not frozen.

I meet Mark on the patio as I'm leaving and he's coming in to start the day. I had the idea that he would have lived somewhere in the hotel but obviously not.

It's a strange thing, when you think about it. You're locked into an establishment for the night with total strangers, the same as at The Bush Inn in New Norfolk and probably the other country pubs I've stayed in, with no-one in charge. I wonder what the situation would be if there was a fire or some other emergency. I guess someone would take over. There's always someone who comes to the fore in a crisis. In fact, I'm quite clear-minded and decisive myself in that situation – it's everyday life *I* find tricky.

'Did you have breakfast?' he asks.

'Yes, I found some cereal and made a cup of tea.' I didn't tell him the tea was to help thaw me out.

'Sleep okay?'

'I was so warm I didn't want to get up.'

'Great.' I take the opportunity to ask him about the two split-timber cottages in the grounds.

'They were used by miners,' he says. 'The one down the back was occupied last night. It's not normally but they begged.' He points to a middle-aged couple loading up their car. 'I told them it was very basic but they came in late and were just happy to have a roof over their heads.' I talk him into posing for me on the patio, giving a personal touch to my photos of the Weldborough Hotel.

***

I'm heading toward a bridge over the Derby River, when I almost fly off the side of the road with surprise. A huge rock, sitting out from the side of the mountain, has been painted as a fish. With green bulbous lips, a large eye and a fin, apparently attached to orange and white scales, it looks, for all the world, like a gigantic grouper. Surrounded by trees, it could, with a bit of imagination, be swimming through water. It's a delightful and eccentric welcome to the gorgeous little ex-mining town of Derby. It's Saturday morning and the town is still asleep. I wander up the street past quaint old miners' cottages and the same buildings that housed the original stores.

A memorial, a statue of a mother and child, stands in front of the *Derby Schoolhouse Museum*. In 1929, after very heavy rain, the Cascade Dam, which provided the mine with water, burst through its wall and the mine and the lower parts of town were suddenly flooded. Fourteen people lost their lives and many horses, used in the mine, were swept away. Perched on a large rock and shaded by trees, it's a poignant reminder of a disaster which must have devastated the community.

I'm often told that what you need in business is a marketing idea that's unique, something that makes you stand out. *The Shop in the Bush* is just that. It's a shop, completely on its own, in the bush. And it's packed with shoppers. Would all these people be in here, looking at antiques and second-hand books if it was in a town? I don't think so. Even I, who hate shopping, can't resist going in. I find a book of photos of Tassie and some local lavender moisturiser. Would I have bought these in a town? No.

Scottsdale is a good-sized town, very vibrant-looking. I stop to visit the Forest Eco Centre, having missed it when I came through on my first trip. It's a weird-looking structure, sort of like a giant fez that has sunk into the ground on one side. This is actually an external shell enabling the building inside to control its own environment. With the aid of air flows and plants and trees acting as bio-mediators, it creates its own microclimate. The centre focuses on the forests and their communities and the history of the North-East, something I've given little thought to so far. I'm keen to have a look but, annoyingly, it's closed. Very strange; I would have thought Saturday was a good day to open something of this nature.

Chapter 26

I planned to bypass Launceston on my way through to my hotel on the Midland Highway but I've followed the wrong sign and ended up, via a detour to *Bridestowe Lavender Farm*, in the middle of the city, with Cataract Gorge on my right. With my hatred of city traffic, I consider allowing myself a mild panic attack, but with Launceston not being the largest of cities, I'm out the other side before I have the chance. On my way through Hadspen, I stop at *Entally House*, a heritage estate I've been trying to see since my trips to Tassie started.

A couple with two children enter at the same time as me and we're welcomed by an extremely friendly and enthusiastic guide. 'I'll start you off in the sitting room,' she says, 'give you a bit of the history of the estate and then I'll leave you to wander.'

And what an interesting history it is. *Entally* was founded in 1819, by Thomas Reiby, the second son of Thomas and Mary Reibey. Thomas 1st had been a junior officer in the East India Company where he had spent time in a suburb of Calcutta called *Entally*, hence the name. Mary Haydock was a convict, having been nabbed as a 13-year-old for the childish prank of disguising herself as a boy and stealing a horse.

'The couple developed successful businesses in farming, trading and shipping along the Hawkesbury River,' says the woman, 'before moving to Sydney to expand. After he died, Mary helped found the first bank in Australia, the Bank of New South Wales, and her image is on the current $20 note.' I make a mental note to check. 'If you've ever been to Circular Quay, you may have noticed a street named after the family. There's also a memorial plaque to Mary in Argyle Street in 'The Rocks'.' The couple smile at each other and nod. 'Thomas 2nd established a branch of the company in Launceston and began building *Entally* in 1819. He died in 1842, and the estate passed to his son, Thomas 3rd.'

This Thomas took a slightly different tack. In 1844, he became the first native Tasmanian to be ordained. He was subject to scandal, when he was accused of 'diverting a lady's affection', and resigned from the church, going into a short spate as a recluse. He returned to the limelight and, as you do when you've been a cleric involved in scandal, went into politics. He served for 30 years, eventually becoming Premier of Tasmania.

The woman gestures toward the window and the sloping lawns surrounding the wide veranda. 'By 1860, the estate included a chapel, conservatory, barns, coach house and coachman's lodge and, most importantly of all, stables.' Thomas was besotted with race horses. Around 90 thoroughbreds were kept at *Entally*. One of those was a horse named *Bagot* which won the *Yan Yean Stakes* at the *Melbourne Cup* Carnival in 1882. Thomas sold the horse later that year, not one of his better decisions. It was renamed *Malua* and won the *Melbourne Cup* in 1884. He must have been tearing his hair out over that one.

'Thomas died in 1912, at the ripe old age of 91. With no heir, the property passed to Thomas Reibey Arthur, the son of his sister, Mary. The Tasmanian Government bought it in 1947, and opened it to the public in 1950. It's an ongoing project,' she says. 'There's not a lot of money allocated so it's a slow process.'

'It's lovely,' I say, to encourage her. The guides in these places are volunteers. They do it because they love the houses and the gardens around them. And they love the history. 'It's so good to be able to come here and see how they actually lived.'

'Yes, well it's our history.'

'Much better than reading it in a book.' She smiles.

'If there's anything you want to know, just ask. I'll be in the staff room down the passage. Enjoy your visit.'

The sitting room is lavishly furnished in cedar. A Georgian chandelier drops from the centre of the ceiling. Old photos are sprinkled around the walls, some going back 120 years. A cricket pitch was put in early on and there's a marvellous photo of the family and friends taking part in a match. The pitch is still in its spot today. It's an unusual house. Tacked onto the back is a second storey with a pitched roof, making that section look just like a doll's house. The top storey houses bedrooms and the bottom floor is a library and large sitting room, specifically for the lord and master. A man needs a shed, they say, and this was Thomas's version, a touch more comfortable and upmarket than the current model.

The gardens, laid out 150 years ago, are still in their original design. A small winery sits on the other side of a fence, separating it from the chapel, the coach house and the stables. A huge Redwood introduces me to an avenue of Dutch Elms and Oak Trees, leading to the coachman's cottage. Trees have flourished all over the property: Pines and Cypress, Cedars, Black Locust and Sweet Bay and just past the front lawn, looking back toward the house, a Giant Sequoia. Mary would be pleased, I'm sure, especially considering it all started with one childish prank.

***

My small motel room in Deloraine has aqua walls, leaf-green trims, forest-green curtains and olive-green bathroom tiles. The doona covers are turquoise, with an ocean motif of fishes and shells. I feel like I've been sucked into an algae-infested swamp. The weather has turned, it's started raining and it's suddenly quite cold. A convection heater sits flat against the wall. It's French – I can tell because there's a button that says 'marche'. I'm guessing that's French for 'go'. I push it but nothing happens. So annoying. Even in my old motel room in Perth last night, everything worked, even the ancient little television that was so small I needed binoculars to watch it. The shower door is stuck open and I rush to shut the front curtain. The window looks straight into the bathroom and I wouldn't inflict that on anyone.

***

During the night the rain receded. I'd left the curtains open to wake to the scene I already know from my last stay here. The sun shines through pink and white clouds, creating light and shadow across the paddocks that lead into the olive-green forest. The snow-speckled peak of Mt. Roland rises, regally, from the greyish-blue of the Western Tiers.

Having discovered Liffey Falls on my last trip, I've decided to look for the township of Liffey. Bob Brown, leader of the Franklin River protest, lives there. I might see if he's at home; I want to thank him. On the way, I stop at the delightful, heritage village of Westbury. It's typically English, even down to its village green. Village greens created an open air meeting place and were used for public celebrations such as May Day. Public punishments were also handed out via the stocks and the whipping post – good Sunday afternoon entertainment for the locals. Surprisingly, the first European settlers were predominantly Irish: ex-convicts, retired soldiers, and free settlers, many of them fleeing the Great Irish Famine of the 1840s. Gaelic was the local language for generations.

The site was surveyed in 1823 and laid out by the *Van Diemen's Land Company* in 1828. Begun as a garrison village, it grew to support the thriving agricultural district surrounding it. Two signs sit at one end of the green:

John Peyton Jones 1809-91 (that's the John Peyton Jones who devised the scheme of a line of vicious dogs at Eaglehawk Neck) *This action secured him legendary status within the convict era. Governor Franklin appointed Jones as Police Magistrate at Westbury in 1841 and he went on to play an important part in the township's early history. He was prominent in local organisations such as the Working*

Men's Club, Public Library, Show Society and St. Andrew's Church and was elected the first warden of the Westbury Municipal Council in 1863. John Peyton Jones is buried in the Westbury Anglican Cemetery.

Westbury nurtured many interesting characters. Two of these were Irish political prisoners, Thomas Francis Meagher and John Mitchel. Meagher and Mitchel helped form the Young Ireland independence movement of the 1840s:

After an abortive rebellion in 1848, they were transported to Van Diemen's Land. The seven young 'Irelanders' were restricted to separate police districts, but this was overcome when Meagher built a cottage at Lake Sorell near where several of the districts met. There they gathered secretly to discuss their dreams for Ireland, their failed revolution and uncertain futures. In 1852, Meagher renounced his parole and escaped through chilling winter conditions over the central plateau to Westbury. Mitchel followed a year later. Both were sheltered by sympathetic Westbury folk and aided on their way to America where they became legendary figures of Irish history. Whoever said Australian history was boring?

I turn south, follow the signs to Liffey and end up on the side of a mountain in the Liffey Forest. I return and follow the signs again, ending up on the side of the same mountain. The town of Liffey does not exist. By lunchtime I'm back in Deloraine, tired and feeling as if I wasted the morning.

Deloraine was opened up in 1821 when grants of farmland were offered to new settlers. The area is now a major agricultural centre. I park the car and wander down the main street, past the beautiful old Deloraine

Hotel, with its miles of stunning iron lacework, and over the bridge. Sculptures by local artists are placed at intervals along the river. Trees shade the beautifully mown lawns, ducks squabble at the water's edge and the river idles by. There's great pride in this lovely town. If you wanted to move to Tassie, this would be a good spot.

Outside the folk museum is a statue of *Malua*, the racehorse that Thomas Reiby lost his hair over. He was bred in 1879 at *Calstock* horse stud, here at Deloraine, and sold to Thomas as a yearling. In 1884, after Thomas had sold him to *Ingleston* in Ballan, Victoria, he won the nation's top races, including the *Newmarket Handicap*, *The Oakleigh Plate*, *The Adelaide Cup* and the *Melbourne Cup*. In 1886, he interrupted a successful stud career to win the *Australian Cup*. If that wasn't enough, he then won the 4800m *Australian Grand National Hurdle* and finally the *Geelong Cup* as a ten-year-old. The locals are pretty proud of their racehorse. Funds were raised in 2007 to build a fitting memorial to 'Australia's Most Versatile Racehorse Ever'.

***

I've always wanted to visit a town with the name of Lower Crackpot. It *has* to be something different. My sister says it reminds her of a man she used to know but that's another story. It is different, as it turns out. It's a miniature village, attached to the large maze and lavender gardens of *Tasmazia*. It was created by Brian Inder. This must be the same Brian Inder who's beautiful poem is engraved on a plaque overlooking the ocean at Arthur River. He seems like a gentle and creative soul. This is his manifesto as the *Laird of Lower Crackpot, Chieftan of Clan Crackpot*:

Here at Tasmazia we do things the Crackpot way. Here fun and laughter rule. Love warms our mountain air. The broad and all-encompassing spirit is the canvas on which we paint our delight in the joy of life. A demanding character, impatience, self-centredness, discourtesy, a mean spirit are not virtues here. They will not be allowed to pollute the sunshine of our day. This is not their place. The eccentric; the artist; the composer; the poet; the writer; the musician and those who love these things; those of a soft and kind nature; those who suffer under the domination of cruder spirits; those who step to a different drum; the loners; the creators; the adventurers; the visionaries; the lovers; the givers and not the takers; the young at heart; the gentle folk. This is their place. May their spirits dwell in eternal summer.

I love miniature villages. My child takes over again, just for a little while. I want to shrink, as Alice does in Wonderland and enter the post office, the fire station, the inn and the church. Vibrant colours are from childhood when there were no rules to follow: pink with turquoise, citrus green with teal, orange, powder blue. I pass *GST House*, the headquarters of the *Liberal Party of Lower Crackpot*, and the ivory tower of the local member, Sir Joh Bjelki Peterson. An upside-down house, an extra wing continuing out from its roof, is *The School of Lateral Thinking*.

The residential area is situated in Upper Lower Crackpot but if you're looking for something a little more down market, *Shirley's Joint*, in lewd salmon pink, *Dirty Shame Saloon*, *Wild Joe's Disco* and the *Ivy Club*, complete with a top hat for a roof, are at the 'sleazy end' of town. Street gas lamps are dotted through gardens and hedgerows. It's a little run down – chips in walls need replastering, some buildings could do with a paint job – but the task of maintaining something like this must be enormous.

I don't dare venture into the maze; I could spend the next two hours lost and panic-stricken, buffeted and scorned by fearless ten-year-olds, maybe even forgotten and locked in for the night. I *did* say my child takes over now and again. I climb a lookout and watch them, enviously, tearing about, wild and free for the moment. Mt. Roland stands as a backdrop, keeping a paternal watch over it all. It's a place of enchantment, paint job or not.

***

The Lighthouse Hotel at Ulverstone is my taste of luxury before going home, though I didn't realise this when I booked. A lovely surprise: huge room, huge bed, huge bathroom, mini-bar, huge television screen. A bargain at $99. Tomorrow night I'm staying in a motel at Latrobe, close to Devonport, to make one last ditch attempt at seeing *Home Hill*, before boarding the ship. Up until then, I'll go where my car leads me.

Chapter 27

It's cold. Mist lies in the valleys and hangs over the paddocks. It quickly disperses, banished by the sun. Hay bales sit in piles in neat green packages. Green hills stretch away, denuded of trees to their halfway mark. Forest, some plantation, some native, covers their crowns. Driveways of pencil pines lead up to white houses. Silver sheds and barns glint in the sunshine. Ragged clouds, white, drift across the pale blue sky to be replaced by others. A kookaburra cackles, crows caw. All is still.

***

The last time I passed through Penguin I was seriously sleep-deprived. This time I can actually *see* what's around me and it's a gorgeous little seaside town, though I would imagine in winter the wind blasting from Bass Strait would make it a little less relaxed and cosy. Penguin was born far away from Tasmania in the Victorian gold rush, which created a demand for timber palings for houses. Locals believe the first settlers were two timber splitters, William Kidd and William Ling. By the end of the 1850s many splitters were working in the surrounding forest. In 1858, James 'Philosopher' Smith, of the Mount Bischoff Mine, discovered copper. A silver mine was also established on the foreshore and operated between 1871 and 1903. So, Penguin was a busy little place for a while.

I have a late lunch of a pastie and coffee at an outdoor table at the bakery. Two boys walk their bikes past me, discussing some 12-year-old subject. They burst into laughter and one shoves the other. A young mother bends over her pram and adjusts the blanket around her toddler, before braving the less sheltered span of pathway. A large camper van trundles past, probably heading for Devonport and The *Spirit*. I wonder if their road trip has been as good as mine.

I down the last of my coffee and wander past an extremely large, fibro-cement penguin, reminding me of a nightmare I had after taking my grandson to a school holiday movie. In fact, you could make a great horror film with a few of these: Hitchcock's *The Birds*, only with bigger – stiffer – birds. It was erected in 1980 to celebrate the centenary of the proclamation of the Penguin township, on 25th October, 1875. I wonder if the members of the memorial committee were all in agreement over this decision or if there were brawls behind the scenes. Maybe I'm just being picky.

I sit on the sea wall and look out toward my home town. I've covered a lot of territory this trip. I've revisited, re-experienced and experienced for the first time. Wherever I go I feel as if I'm somewhere familiar, from the wildness of the west coast to the ethereal beauty of the east; craggy Mt. Roland and the Western Tiers to the Blue Tiers of the North-East; the quaintness and charm of the Heritage Highway, the grim history of the Tasman

Peninsula and the elegance of Hobart and Launceston. It occurs to me that I've only scraped the surface. It also occurs to me that there's no way I could not come back and keep scraping. One day, I will brave the South-West Wilderness but for that I'll need a 'real' car. In the meantime, there's Savage River, the *Milkshake Hills Forest Drive* in the South Arthur forests of the Tarkine, and the islands: Bruny, Maria, Flinders and King. Arthur River is dragging at me to return and watch a summer sunset.

Would it be easier – and cheaper – just to shift here? It wouldn't. If I decided to up stakes, to leave my birth place at last, it would be to go north, closer to the sun. I can only handle cold in short bursts and even Melbourne is a challenge in winter. Tassie is better left as a gift, a reminder of the earth around me that's so easily forgotten in the hype, pollution and man-made constructs of a big city. With limited phone connection, little radio and often no television set at the end of the day, it's a self-imposed retreat, allowing my Spirit to rest, regroup and begin again, fresh.

And then there's the exploring. I'm never bored; each day shows me something new. Sitting in my miners' hotel in Weldborough, surrounded by rain forest, woken by kookaburras, the rustling of trees and an odd bird call I'm yet to identify, I felt as if I was in the middle of nowhere. And yet Scottsdale is a mere 20 minutes away and the city of Launceston, just an hour further on. The West Coast and the East Coast could be in two different countries and the modernity of the cities contrasts sharply with the vestiges of their dark beginnings.

***

The morning traffic roars around the huge roundabout on the highway next door to my motel in Latrobe. It's a bit different to waking to kookaburras.

'Good morning,' says a woman's voice, '*Spirit of Tasmania*. How may I help you?'

'I'm booked on the boat for tonight,' I say, 'in a recliner.'

'Yes?'

'I'm looking for an upgrade to a share cabin.'

'One moment, please. I'll check for you.' After 15 days of almost non-stop moving, I need to spend the trip home in a bed, asleep. It will probably add $80 to the price – that's the extra they were going to charge me when I booked the trip – but it's only money.

'Yes,' says the woman, 'I can put you in a four berth.'

'How much extra will that be?'

'Let me see. I can do that for $43.' And that's a lesson learnt. Book a recliner and upgrade later, for half the price. I'm enormously relieved to have a bunk for tonight. I wonder if there will be four of us in there. Four strangers in a small cabin? Now *that* will be interesting.

***

Latrobe and I have a history. Whatever I plan doesn't come off. I've started my last morning here, specifically to return to the *Courthouse Museum*. I remember it as being a terrific display of the town's history and I wanted another look. It never occurred to me to check opening times, which is ridiculous, because I've learnt to do that to avoid this exact situation. Who'd have thought, though, that a museum in the centre of town wouldn't open till 1pm? I revisit *Anvers Chocolate Factory* on the way out. It's impossible to pass this place without stopping, and I shout myself some extremely expensive, extremely delicious, bits and pieces. I recommend the chocolate truffles.

A sign points out that Port Sorell, a place I've only seen in the depths of winter during a downpour, is just 19 kilometres up the road. Why not have another look? I've got loads of time, seeing that Latrobe has let me down again. On the way the phone rings, giving me a shock. It's the first time it's rung since I arrived. Most of my family now realise that ringing me in the wilds of Tassie is a waste of their time, and catch up with the news when I get back.

'Hi, Grandma.' My 15-year-old grandson is going out for lunch near my home with his father and my other son. His voice crackles in and out. 'Do you want to come?'

'I'm in Tassie.'

'Pardon?'

'I'm on a trip to Tassie. I won't be home till Friday.' The phone cuts out and I swear. It's ridiculous that I'm on the Bass Strait coast and can't receive a call from the *opposite* coastline. I try returning the call but it drops out as soon as he answers. I send a text explaining where I am and apologise for the uselessness of my phone. I have no idea if he received it.

Port Sorell is a very happy place. Whether it's the sunshine, the holiday feel or the closeness of the bay area, everyone seems to be smiling. New estates are sprouting from the ground, brand new houses, some, my idea of mansions. Maybe retirees are choosing Port Sorell.

I don't blame them. It would be a great spot to retire to, 20 minutes from Devonport and only an hour from Launceston.

The beach looks out over the Rubicon Estuary. The estuary is fed by several streams, including the Franklin Rivulet and the Rubicon River. It is bounded by the town on the west, Narawntapu National Park on the north-east and pasture on the east and south. A light breeze ripples the turquoise water. The olive-green of the hills on the other side of the estuary morphs gradually into lavender-tinted mountains. Wispy white clouds streak the bluest of skies.

Huge copper-coloured rocks litter this part of the shoreline. They're encased in something strange and I move closer to see what it is. Millions of miniature black shells cling to the rocks, all but covering some of them. I gently draw one off but it's stuck fast. It's one of the weirdest things I've ever seen, like something out of science fiction. At any moment I expect them to come swarming off to envelop and devour me.

Chapter 28

'You're lucky you came now,' says the woman, as she shows a couple out the door. 'I was about to close up.' I can't believe I was within a minute of missing out on *Home Hill* for the third time. I thought I knew where it was and I was expecting to go straight to it. It wasn't there, though, (my excuse is that I'm tired from 15 days of driving) and I'd spent an hour and a half running around Devonport, looking for it. Devonport's Visitor Centre was going to bail me out but it's now a bank.

'It's been a bank for years,' the young woman said, 'You must have an old map.'

'Yes, I guess it is old. So where has the Visitor Centre shifted to?'

'There isn't one.'

'There isn't one? Devonport hasn't got a Visitor Centre?'

'There's a tourist map on a board at the back of the supermarket.'

'Does anyone here know where *Home Hill* is?' I asked, scanning the other teller and two customers. They waved their heads, vaguely, as if they'd never heard of it. Time was running out – the house closed at four and it was now a quarter to three. I rushed to the back of the supermarket but *Home Hill* isn't on the board. Dashing back up the long main street to the car to feed the parking meter, I popped my head into a *Just Jeans* store, on the off-chance someone in there could give me a clue.

'*Home Hill*,' said the young man behind the counter, 'I'll show you.' I could have kissed him (I didn't but I could have). He drew a little map and ran his pen along the road leading to my quarry. In fact, I had been within an inch of it, an hour ago, before turning back thinking I was on the wrong track. Needless to say, the thought that, after all this, the guide might have gone home early, was almost too much.

'I thought I was here in plenty of time,' I say to her.

'No, tours are at two o'clock and after that we go home.'

'But the website says you're open till four.'

'Yes,' she says, 'they'll have to do something about that.' We both know, in this moment, that that's not going to happen. I break the silence.

'This is my third time trying to see this place. Last time, these same hours were not just on the website but on your door and still no-one was here.'

'Gosh,' she says, 'my hands have gone all cold,' and I realise my anger is upsetting her. It's reasonable to *be* angry. It makes sense to organise your last day around the sites in Devonport. If the guides decide not to hang around or not to turn up at all, it's too late to plan something else.

'Still, I'm here,' I say, taking a couple of deep breaths. 'I've been doing some research on Dame Enid and she seemed like a fabulous woman.'

'Oh yes, she was.' She stops ringing her hands and relaxes into her spiel.

The house is not at all stately, as I expected, but something for a normal family to come home to. Various extensions lead off in different directions, added as more children were born. The final count was 12. It surprises me to learn that Sir Joseph was not well paid, as you would expect a Prime Minister to be, and so it must have been a job to keep it all going. Many of the pieces of furniture are the originals used by the family, which adds to its cosiness. There's a sense that they were only recently here. The woman points out the lampshades.

'Enid made those because she couldn't find what she wanted.'

'So she was domestic as well as political?'

'Oh, yes. Once I had a woman say how much she liked some wallpaper. But it wasn't wallpaper. It was a frieze, painted by Enid to disguise cracks that had appeared when the road was being put in. She could do anything.'

The rooms are packed with a mind-boggling display of historical memorabilia: photos, gifts, ornaments bought on overseas trips, and plaques. 'The cup on the top shelf was presented to Joe on a visit to Ireland,' she says. 'He was Irish *and* Catholic, you know, so they loved him in Ireland. And the rose vase was given to Enid for fundraising for the *Red Cross*. As representative of the public service she was 'Queen for the Day' and her page boy was a young Errol Flynn.' I peer at the beautiful youth in the photo.

'This clock is from when Joe opened the first *Holden* car factory at Fisherman's Bend in Victoria.' It's adorable how she speaks of this couple as if they were personal friends and had only recently passed on. Sir Joe and Dame Enid had that ability to relate with everyday people as equals and Devonport locals, in particular, feel a personal connection with them. They were an ordinary family and accepted on these terms by ordinary people. Except they weren't ordinary, obviously.

'This gentleman, the Duke of Gloucester,' she points to another photo, 'was the Governor-General of Australia. He was the brother of *King George VI*.'

'But didn't the King's brother abdicate for Wallis Simpson?'

'No, the younger brother, Henry.' Of course, there were other brothers. It's easy to forget that, they've had so little air play. 'And this couch ... Joe nearly died in a car accident when he was Premier of Tasmania.'

'I didn't realise that.'

'Yes. That's where he made his recovery. You can see it's been well used. A group from Hobart got together and bought him another car. Of course, with a broken leg he couldn't drive it so Enid had to learn to drive in a week to bring him home.' This woman's pedestal is rising by the minute. 'You can imagine what *that* would have been like in the 30s. The roads would still have been dirt, wouldn't they?'

'I guess so,' I reply. She moves across to a glass cabinet.

'Now, this spoon was given to Enid by Neville Chamberlain's wife. It's a copy of the anointing spoon of *George VI* – the original would have been gold, as all royal things were gold, weren't they – and the gold scissors cut the ribbon for the Port Pirie to Port Augusta train line. They got to keep the gifts,' she adds. They got to keep the gifts and so they were surrounded by beautiful things but had trouble paying the bills. 'When Enid was in England in 1935 for the Silver Jubilee, she wrote articles for the newspapers. She was quite excited. She got paid for those.' Was there anything this woman couldn't do? 'And that's a signed autograph of Elizabeth and Albert, from 1927. That's before he was *George VI*.'

I'm going into information overload. I wish she'd leave me for a little while to wander by myself. She's not going to, though.

'What happened with all the children, I wonder? Boarding schools, I guess.'

'The older ones went off to school. After all, there wasn't room at the Lodge.'

'No?'

'No, the Lodge only has four bedrooms.' You assume the leaders of countries live in luxury but not necessarily, certainly not in Australia. I don't suppose it entered their heads when building the Lodge that it would be descended on by a family of 14. In the main bedroom is a beautiful carved bed. 'That was Joe's father's bed, brought from the family home in Stanley. We're very lucky. Before Enid died, she sold the house to the *Devonport Council* and gave all these contents to the *National Trust*. The family weren't happy at the time but if she hadn't, we wouldn't have this legacy.'

'Well, a lot of this stuff was given to him as the representative of Australia, so you could see it as belonging to the country rather than the family.'

'Yes. The Council cares for the grounds and The *National Trust* looks after the house and the contents.

That's Joe's headstone out there,' she points through a latticed window into the garden, 'and the ashes of Garnet, the baby that only lived a few months.'

'I didn't realise she'd lost a baby.'

'Yes,' she says, gazing for a moment out the window. 'You knew that after Joe died Enid had a breakdown?'

'I didn't.' Well-deserved, I'd say. I would have had it while he was alive, just to make sure he knew how hard I'd been working, including living through 11 pregnancies with a fractured pelvis.

'I won't take you past there,' she says, pointing to a door, 'because they're the offices.' At this stage, I wish she wouldn't take me anywhere. It's been very interesting, for sure. She's extremely professional and knowledgeable but I'm desperate to get by myself for the short time that's left. The running of heritage estates is interesting. Some tours are very relaxed, as at *Entally*, where you are left to explore at will, and others, highly controlled, where you are not allowed out of sight. Understandable here, I guess. This house and its contents are so valuable in terms of their historical legacy, they wouldn't want any of it to go missing. Still, do I look like the sort of person who would slip a *Royal Doulton* plate or an ivory nun into my pocket? Maybe I do. I thank her for looking after the house so well. There's a hint of relief as she closes the door. I've put her into overtime.

***

It's dusk and a huge crowd is already waiting at the docks. I pull up beside what looks like a large group of *MG* enthusiasts. There must have been some sort of Easter rally. They stand around together, laughing and talking animatedly. Children skip up and down between the cars and a little white spaniel strains at its leash to join them. There's a relaxed, party atmosphere here.

I jump the queue and am first into the cabin, allowing me to shower before my bed mates arrive. Just as I finish, the door rattles open and a large woman enters and looks around shyly. She's been allotted the top bunk and I feel sorry for her as she drags her bag and her bulk up the ladder. I gather she booked ages ago and annoyance flicks across her face when I drop the 'clanger' that I didn't book until this morning. That's another lesson learnt – change your booking at the last moment and end up with a bottom bunk.

'Do you live in Tassie?' I ask her.

'I live at Lake Leake, between Swansea and Campbell Town.'

'How lovely.' I haven't been there yet but I know it would be.

'It is. I've been there six years now.'

'You're not from Tassie then?'

'No, Melbourne.'

'And you're happy there?'

'Oh yes, it's beautiful. Every night I have a deer that comes and chomps on the bushes outside my window.'

'I'm so jealous.' Actually, I'm green with envy. I must check out Lake Leake next time.

Next time. How easily that came. Suddenly, it's not whether I'll come back but when. As a teenager I stood looking out across the bay and all I wanted to do was get on a ship and go over the horizon to see what was on the other side. Tassie's on the other side. The rest of the world is on the other side as well – *and* the rest of Australia. That's where my challenge lies. How do I explore the rest of Australia, the country that I love and have seen only snippets of, England, from where my ancestors originated and whose history, films and books I grew up with, Europe, and anywhere else that offers itself as irresistible, and still fit in an annual fortnight in the forests of my island? I leave that one hanging for the moment, buy an exceedingly rough but now ritualistic red wine and sit out on the deck. The engines throb and the ship eases away from the dock and starts its turn. Darkness falls as we glide along the river. A group of seven or eight people stand on the beach waving. I wave back, pretending it's to them. But it's not.

'Bye, Tassie. See you soon.'

≈

About the Author

Coral Waight started travelling alone at the age of sixty. She began by crossing Bass Strait, south of where she lives in Melbourne, Australia, to explore the island state of Tasmania. After four road trips around the forests, caves and coastlines of her beloved 'Tassie', she ventured further afield, across the Tasman Sea to New Zealand, with its fiords, glaciers, volcanic valleys and its *Lord of the Rings* trail. With these experiences under her belt, she took the leap to the other side of the world. England provided Dickens, the Brontes and Shakespeare; medieval cities and West End theatres; a malevolent rental car, indecipherable road signs and menacing roundabouts. Her *Planning to the Nth* series describes the challenges, pitfalls – and joys – of a woman, 'of an age', discovering the world – at last.

Coral can be found at:
www.facebook.com/coral.waight
or her travel blog:
coralwaightravel.com

www.ingramcontent.com/pod-product-compliance
Lightning Source LLC
Chambersburg PA
CBHW051940290426
44110CB00015B/2048